Magic Numbers for Stock Investors

Magic Numbers for Stock Investors

How To Calculate the 25 Key Ratios for Investing Success

Peter Temple

John Wiley & Sons (Asia) Pte Ltd

Other Wiley Editorial Offices

John Wiley & Sons, Inc., 111 River Street, Hoboken, NJ07030, USA
John Wiley & Sons Ltd, The Atrium, Southern Gate, Chichester P019 8SQ, UK
John Wiley & Sons (Canada) Ltd, 22 Worcester Road, Rexdale, Ontario M9W 1L1, Canada
John Wiley & Sons Australia Ltd, 33 Park Road (PO Box 1226), Milton, Queensland 4064, Australia
Wiley-VCH, Pappelallee 3, 69469 Weinheim, Germany

Library of Congress Cataloging-in-Publication Data
0-470-82124-8 (cloth)

Typeset in 12/14 points, Times Roman by Linographic Services Pte Ltd
Printed in Singapore by Saik Wah Press Pte Ltd
10 9 8 7 6 5 4 3 2

Contents

Foreword

Magic Numbers for Stock Investors really are magic. They help investors understand what is behind the screen of often confusing and misleading company financial statements. With this well-organized book, both the new investor and the experienced analyst have a comprehensive explanation of the key financial ratios which are critical to understanding company finances and making better-informed investment decisions. As the author points out, the recent accounting scandals in the United States and other parts of the world, particularly the emerging markets world, have not resulted in a dramatic improvement. Investors thus need the "magic numbers" more than ever before.

The author does an excellent job of reviewing the many commonly used ratios but also discloses some unique and innovative ratios which are less commonly used but which promise to help analysts further improve their understanding of company finances. For example PRR (price to research spending) along with the sales, earnings and equity-per-share ratios are particularly interesting. Each ratio is clearly explained with: definition, formulas, components, where to find the data, the calculation theory, a specific company example, and how to interpret the results.

While reading the book, I found myself underlining various explanations and definitions that clarified a number of points and, more importantly, identified various benchmarks. It's a book that should be on every investor's bookshelf not only as a reference but as a tool to be continuously used.

Mark Mobius
Managing Director, Templeton Emerging Markets Fund
Author of *Passport to Profits* and *Mobius on Emerging Markets*

More "Magic Numbers" – How They Can Help You

In the introduction to the original *Magic Numbers* book, I posed a series of questions to the reader. Have you ever looked at a newspaper report that used financial jargon and wondered what it meant? Have you ever wished that you knew how to interpret a set of company accounts? Have you ever thought there must be an easy way to get a "feel" for the value of a company by doing a few simple calculations?

The original "lucky" 33 ratios were never going to encompass all of the possible stock market ratios I could have included.

So this book is the first of a series of follow-ups that will focus more intently on how different categories of users can use "magic numbers" in their investment and trading. This book has 25 ratios that are particularly relevant for stock investors. A follow-up book will have 25 ratios useful for bond and derivatives investors.

What does *Magic Numbers for Stock Investors* include? There are some ratios that I included in the original book, but in these cases some of the text has been rewritten, and new and updated examples have been used, primarily of large international companies.

While I have retained some of the key *valuation ratios* that were included in the original *Magic Numbers*, I have included a couple of additional ones: EV to sales and the price to research ratio. I have assumed that readers are familiar with price earnings ratios and dividend yields, and so have not included these most basic of ratios that were in any case covered in the original. But I have kept price to sales, price to book, and several other key measures.

With the exception of a reprise of margins, all of the *income statement ratios* take the analysis that I introduced in the original book to a more detailed level. So I have assumed, for example, that readers will be familiar with interest and dividend cover. But I've included in this section a detailed look at sales, earnings and equity per share, and how they interact, at sales and profit per employee, and ratios that look at remuneration of staff and management. I think all these ratios are useful ones to investigate.

Cash flow ratios include, as did the original *Magic Numbers* book, discounted cash flow and price to cash flow, as well as the operating cash flow to operating profit ratio. I think these do bear some repetition. But we have also added a couple of new ones: free cash flow to sales and cash flow return on invested capital. Both have been proved to be key determinants of future share price movements in research conducted by leading investment banks, and I think that all investors need to know about them. Once again, where ratios are repeated from the original, some text has changed, and wholly new examples are included.

Finally, the *balance sheet ratios* section reprises several key balance sheet numbers included in the original, complete with up-to-date examples. I have also added, in a two-part section, the balance sheet analysis tool known as the Z-score. This is an important measure of future financial solvency.

As did the original, *Magic Numbers for Stock Investors* strips away the jargon. It uses simple examples from real company accounts and other relevant data, and shows you how to calculate these 25 key ratios that really matter when valuing a company's shares, checking out its financial standing, and looking at its profitability.

You don't need to be an accountant or a high-level mathematician to read this book. Any accounting terminology used in the book is explained in easy-to-understand terms.

As before, all you will need is a basic grasp of how numbers and arithmetic work, an inquiring mind, and the ability to use a calculator.

THE "MAGIC NUMBERS" CONCEPT, COMPANIES, AND THE STOCK MARKET

In one of those strokes of luck that authors and publishers can only hope will happen, the original *Magic Numbers* was published at a time when concern about accounting issues was at its height.

Since the Enron and Worldcom debacles, and what these events demonstrated about the general state of accounting and stock market valuation techniques, much greater attention has since been paid to the objective measures that investors can and should use to work out whether or not a company's accounts displays the necessary levels of integrity.

But if investors had thought that companies would be chastened by the accounting scandals, they might have been mistaken. When I started some of the preliminary work for this book, the headlines were full of news that companies in the United States and elsewhere had been manipulating projected pension fund returns to bolster current profits. In other words, skepticism is still warranted. One famous UK short-seller advises investors to treat every statement made in a company report and accounts as a lie, unless it can be proved otherwise.

The upshot is that investors need to use this expanded and refocused list of "magic numbers" more than ever. All of them can be worked out, using a simple pocket calculator, from share prices and other data available from a good quality business newspaper, from information provided by companies in their official accounts, or from other easily available resources.

At the end of this book are some details of how to obtain basic corporate information from print sources and from financial web sites. Such web sites operated by companies themselves can be a useful source of basic information. Many provide an online version of their official accounts. Where necessary, I've indicated in the text where specialist print information web sites need to be used.

There is one important point here. Don't take accounting ratios provided by web or print-based statistical services as being entirely reliable. Definitions do vary, although moves are being made to develop consistent international accounting standards. Remember that there is no substitute for calculating these "magic numbers" yourself.

As with the original book, some of the worksheets used in *Magic Numbers for Stock Investors* are available on the Web (a selection is available at *www.magicnumbersbook.com*) for you to download and use, at your own risk, as you see fit. The web site also includes worksheets applicable to the ratios in the original book. Other useful web addresses are in the appendix at the end of this book.

How this book is organized

I've grouped each set of these new "magic numbers for stock investors" sections into a logical sequence. As explained above, they look in turn at:

- Valuation "magic numbers" – mainly calculated using share price, market capitalization, and items from the company's profit and loss account or income statement.

- Income statement "magic numbers" – calculated using data from the company's profit and loss account.

- Cash flow statement "magic numbers" – calculated from the various components of the flows of cash into and out of the business.

- Balance sheet "magic numbers" – calculated from the balance sheet statement of a company's assets and liabilities.

Each section contains an overview of the ratios and how they are used. Each of the 25 "magic number" sections is organized in the same way. The sections contain:

- a definition of the "magic number" in words and symbols

- a definition of its components

- where to find the information needed to calculate it

- a theoretical example of how to calculate it

- an actual example of how to calculate it

- the significance of the "magic number" and how to interpret it.

WILL YOU USE *MAGIC NUMBERS FOR STOCK INVESTORS* IN THE FUTURE?

Once again I can guarantee that you will! Recent volatile markets means that making money is hard. Researching companies in depth before you buy is the only way of having the comfort you are picking sound investments. Not only that, but turbulent markets have meant that investors are considering alternatives to traditional stock market investments and seeking ways to avoid assuming unnecessary risk.

Accountants are increasingly getting together to make companies conform to a single global standard. This means that knowing what the numbers mean – and the nuances involved in their calculation – can give you an investing edge. Most importantly, it can tell you what companies and what types of investment vehicle to avoid.

THANKS TO ...

Nick Wallwork, my publisher at Wiley Asia, for sparking the original idea for the "magic numbers" series and turning it into profitable reality.

Janis Soo, my editor at Wiley Asia, for shepherding the book to publication.

Edward Caruso for copyediting, proofreading, and valuable comments on content.

Richard Howard, for patiently "auditing" the calculations in the original book.

Lynn Temple, for her commentary on the book's content and for checking for errors at final proof stage, and for researching and writing the appendix.

A LAST WORD

As in the previous book, I have to urge readers to be both careful and skeptical! Accounting policies do differ. Even where they don't, companies have considerable latitude as to how they interpret them. If a "magic number" looks unduly different from one calculated for the same company for a previous year, or for the same ratio at another company, check to see if there is a reason.

The reason may be an accounting policy change, or just a quirk of the figures. The real reason may not be obvious. It could be buried in the small print of the accounts. Detective work may be required.

Anomalies do arise, and often present outstanding investment opportunities. But equally, they can signify "creative" accounting that could conceal potential problems. If the accounts seem unduly complex, like Enron's were, be suspicious. With experience, you will be able to distinguish between the profitable anomaly and the danger signals.

I hope you enjoy *Magic Numbers for Stock Investors*. But do read it in conjunction with the original *Magic Numbers*. It will give you an overview of most of the key numbers needed for successful and profitable long-term investment in the stock markets of the world.

Part One

Valuation "Magic Numbers"

Valuation "Magic Numbers"

In each of the seven ratios contained in this section, I look at how a share price can be combined with measurements from a company's income statement and balance sheet. We can use them in order to assess whether or not a stock is cheap or expensive.

To repeat the quote from Oscar Wilde in the original *Magic Numbers*, a cynic is "a man who knows the price of everything and the value of nothing." Investors should not fall into this trap. There is no shortage of cynics in the stock market. However, any investor who confuses price with value will probably lose money.

Simply because a share has a low price does not necessarily mean it is a bargain. Similarly, a share with a high nominal price may not be expensive. It is easy to grasp that stock prices have to be compared with sales, profits and profit growth, and asset data to have meaning.

The following seven "magic numbers for stock investors" relate the stock market price of a share to similar data from the company's accounts, and allow you to distinguish effectively between price and value.

- The price to sales ratio (PSR) compares the stock market value of the company with its annual turnover or revenue.

- Price to book value (P/BV) looks at the relationship between the market value of the company and its assets.

- EV/EBITDA compares the "enterprise value" (EV) of the business (this is its stock market value adjusted for debt and cash) with its operating profits before deducting charges such as interest and tax, and book entries like depreciation and amortization.

- EV to sales is another measure that uses enterprise value, this time comparing it with sales. Once again it is used for international and inter-company comparisons.

- Price-earnings growth (PEG) factors relate price-earnings ratios to recent or expected growth in profits earned. They add an extra dimension to the humble PE ratio.

- The price to research spending ratio (PRR) is useful for companies that are science or technology based, and that spend large quantities on research and development (R&D). The ratio measures how much R&D investors are buying per pound, euro or dollar invested.

- Finally in this section, reinvested return on equity (RROE), featured in the original *Magic Numbers*, is reprised here. It combines several important elements in share valuation, including return on equity, the amount paid out in dividends, and market benchmarks like the risk-free rate of return, as a way of deducing whether a company is cheap or expensive.

These "magic numbers" are some of the common, and also some of the less well-known, ways in which shares can be valued. Each has its own importance and each can be given more or less weight, depending on the type of company being valued. All the ratios have a proven track record in identifying undervalued and overvalued businesses.

For those companies with consistent growth, PEGs and reinvested return on equity may be the best.

For companies making losses, or whose profits are relatively low – perhaps because of high levels of depreciation, amortization, or other book entries – EV/EBITDA and EV to sales are often used as yardsticks. They can also be used to make cross-border comparisons of companies in the same industry, or to compare companies with different capital structures.

Remember, however, that none of these measures should be viewed in isolation from the underlying figures from which they are derived, or from other "magic numbers" in this book.

By way of example, take the PSR. Price to sales ratios will be lower for companies – such as supermarket chains or investment banks – running businesses that have high turnover, but make relatively low profits as a percentage of those sales.

"Price to book" is a good yardstick to use for assessing asset-based companies, but care needs to be taken over identifying how the assets in question have been valued. Price to research is used only for science- or technology-based companies.

The sections that follow examine each of these seven "magic numbers" in more depth. Read on to find out how to get the data you need, how to calculate them, and what they mean.

1

Price to Sales Ratio

THE DEFINITION

The *price to sales ratio (PSR)* is sometimes known as the "revenue multiple." It is the market capitalization of the shares divided by the company's annual sales. An alternative definition is share price divided by sales per share. Other common terms for sales are "turnover" or "revenue."

THE FORMULAS

PSR = market capitalization/annual sales

or

PSR = share price/sales per share

THE COMPONENTS

Market capitalization – this is the stock market value of the company. You calculate it by multiplying the total of issued shares (or common stock) outstanding by their price.

In turn, the components of this calculation are: *issued shares (common stock) outstanding* – shares that have been issued and are capable of being publicly traded; and the *share (stock) price* – the current market price of the shares, normally the mid-market price at the close of business on the previous trading day.

Annual sales – sales, revenue, and turnover are virtually inter-changeable terms. They are in such common use as to need little further explanation. Where calculations differ is usually in whether or not, in performing this calculation, you take the sales for the last reported year, or the last 12 months.

Using the figures for the last 12 months is common practice for US companies, because they report quarterly. In this case, the figure to take (assuming a forecast is not used) is the cumulative sales for the preceding four reported quarters. In other words, if a company has recently announced third-quarter sales, the sales figures for the last 12 months would be the sales for the nine months of the current year added to the fourth quarter of the previous one.

In the same way, for companies reporting twice yearly, if a half-year has been reported, sales in the first half of the current year would be added to those of the second half of the previous one.

In all other cases the last reported full-year sales figure is the correct one to use.

WHERE'S THE DATA?

Annual sales – normally this is the topmost figure or subtotal in the consolidated profit and loss account or income statement. Any sales deriving from large one-off business disposals may distort the figure. They should be excluded. Quarterly and "last 12 months" sales figures for US and other companies can usually be found on web-based news services such as Yahoo! Finance (*http:// finance.yahoo.com*).

Issued shares outstanding (in order to calculate market capit-alization) – in the notes to the accounts. The note can usually be found from a reference in the consolidated balance sheet next to the heading, "called-up share capital" or a similar term. The number of ordinary shares at the end of the year should be taken, and not their stated nominal money value.

Share (stock) price (in order to calculate market capitalization) – from any daily financial newspaper or financial web site. Care should be taken to use the actual share price. Note also that financial newspapers often include individual company's market capitalizations on their share price pages.

CALCULATING IT – THE THEORY

Figure 1.1 shows the different numbers to be pulled from the accounts and how to use them to calculate the ratio.

Figure 1.1 Calculating the "Magic Number" for PSR (half-yearly reporting)

Universal Widgets plc has a sales progression as follows:

	Six months to:		Year to
	Jun-03	**Jun-02**	**Dec-02**
Sales (£m)	120	100	200
It has issued shares of …	200m		
… and a share price of …	100p		
Last 12 months sales are …	£220m		
(working)	(200 + 120 − 100)		
Market capitalization is …	£200m		
(working – in £)	200 × (100/100)		
PSR is …	**0.91**		
(working)	(200/220)		

Calculating the "Magic Number" for PSR (quarterly reporting)

Universal Widgets Inc. reports quarterly. Its quarterly pattern of sales is:

	2002 Q1	2002 Q2	2002 Q3	2002 Q4	2003 Q1
Revenue ($m)	50	75	75	100	125
It has issued shares of …	200m				
… and a stock price of …	$10				
Last 12 months sales are …	$375m				
(working)	(75 + 75 + 100 + 125)				
Market capitalization is …	$2,000m				
(working)	(200 × 10)				
PSR (or "revenue multiple") …	**5.3**				
(working)	(2,000/375)				

The example shows two ways of calculating the number. They are applicable respectively to companies that report half-yearly and those that report quarterly. In the case of companies whose full year has just been reported, the calculation of the denominator is easy – simply take the annual figure straight from the accounts.

CALCULATING IT FOR
GLAXOSMITHKLINE (GSK)

Figure 1.2 shows how the highlighted numbers from this extract from the accounts of GSK combine to produce the "magic number". More information is on the company's web site at *www.gsk.com*. Glaxo is a leading global pharmaceutical company.

Figure 1.2   Calculating it from GlaxoSmithKline's 2002 accounts

The figures ...

Financial summary (restated)	2002 £m	2001 £m
Sales	21,212	20,489

Note 27

Share capital issued and fully paid		
At 31st December	6,024.27m	
Share price	£12.51	

The calculations ...

Market capitalization	£75,364m	
(working)	(6,024.27 × 12.51)	
PSR	**3.55**	
(working)	(75,364/21,212)	

In this instance, calculating the market capitalization is fairly straightforward. Take care, however, to express the result in terms that are the same as those used to express the sales figure (millions comparing with millions, and so on). For many companies, this requires some care to be taken when calculating market capitalization. In GSK's case, however, with a share price expressed in pounds, the calculation becomes relatively simple.

WHAT IT MEANS

Though once unloved, the PSR became increasingly used in the late 1990s as investors, or rather analysts and investment bankers, realized that it could be used to provide a valuation measure, however tenuous, for companies with no foreseeable prospect of making a profit.

Hence, it was used extensively to value Internet and telecoms companies, especially using *forecasts* of revenue rather than historic audited figures. As movements in the prices of some of these shares have shown, this meant greater attention was paid to whether or not these companies met quarterly sales forecasts, and with sharp downward movements in the stock price if they didn't.

This method of valuing companies has now been thoroughly discredited, not least because some companies were shown to have artificially inflated turnover to pander to investor expectations.

There is some justification, in the same way as with price-earnings ratios and earnings growth, for companies that can demonstrate high and consistent levels of sales revenue growth to sell on higher multiples than those whose sales are static or growing more slowly. This is far, however, from being a hard and fast rule.

Cold reality is more mundane. The PSR can be used as a way of assessing the cheapness or otherwise of the shares. But there is a catch. The normal rule of thumb is simple. Companies that have a PSR of significantly less than one can be considered cheap: those that haven't are expensive.

There is a respectable body of evidence to suggest that this rule works.

In his book *What Works on Wall Street*, James O'Shaughnessy examined US share price and accounts data for an extended part of the postwar period and found that a historic PSR of less than one was the most reliable indicator of the future share price performance of companies. It is therefore an indicator that pays to look at closely when assessing whether a stock is cheap or expensive.

2

Price to Book Value

THE DEFINITION

This *price to book value (P/BV) ratio* is often called by the shorthand term "price to book." It is the share price divided by the book value of the shares. Book value is the value of the net assets attributable to shareholders expressed as a per-share figure.

THE FORMULA

P/BV = share price/(stockholders' equity/no. of shares in issue)

THE COMPONENTS

Share (stock) price – the current market price of the shares, normally the mid-market price at the close of business on the previous trading day.

Book value – this goes by a number of different names, including stockholders' or shareholders' equity, shareholders' funds, net assets, and net tangible assets. Take the figure that represents the tangible fixed assets of the business, plus its current assets. Deduct all current liabilities, long-term creditors, and provisions. The residual is the assets that are "owned" by shareholders.

Issued shares (common stock) outstanding – shares that have been issued and are capable of being publicly traded. Use the shares outstanding at the point in time the calculation is performed for the calculation. You can get these numbers from the annual report, but they need to be adjusted for any subsequent share issue or stock split.

WHERE'S THE DATA?

Share (stock) price – from any daily newspaper or financial web site. Take note of the units in which the share price is expressed. In the United Kingdom, shares are traditionally quoted in pence, so to arrive at a market capitalization expressed in pounds, the price must be adjusted accordingly when you do the calculation.

Book value – this is on the face of the consolidated balance sheet normally using one of the alternative phrases listed earlier. You can also identify it as the total of share capital and reserves. Take care to exclude, if they are present, any intangible assets or goodwill. Intangible assets should only be included if they have been developed by, and are integral to, the business. Examples where this is appropriate include customer lists, publishing titles, copyright on intellectual property like software, and some popular consumer brand names.

Issued shares (common stock) outstanding – these are in the notes to the accounts. You can find the note from a reference in the consolidated balance sheet next to the heading, "called-up share capital" or a similar term. Use the number of ordinary shares at the end of the year, and not their stated nominal money value.

The number of shares used to calculate earnings per share should *not* be used. This will normally be an average for the year, not the most recent year-end figure. In this instance, the most recent figure is the one to use, because it corresponds with the net assets figure. This is also worked out at the end of the year.

CALCULATING IT – THE THEORY

Figure 2.1 shows the different numbers to be pulled from the accounts and how to use them to calculate the ratio.

Figure 2.1   Calculating the "Magic Number" for price/book value

Consolidated Flanges has …	
A share price of …	200p
Shareholders' equity of …	£600m
Shares outstanding of …	400m
Book value per share (in pence) is … (working)	150p (600/400) × 100
Price to book is … (working)	**1.33** (200/150)

Figure 2.2 shows how the highlighted numbers from this extract from the accounts of Sony for the year to March 2002 combine to produce the "magic number." Sony is a major global consumer electronics group and a film, software, and music publisher. More information on the company is at *www.sony.com*. For simplicity, I have taken the numbers stated in the accounts in US dollars, as this avoids the large unwieldy numbers generated when using Japanese yen in the calculation.

Figure 2.2   Calculating price/book value from Sony's accounts

The figures ...

Consolidated financial information 2002	Year to March 31, 2002
Consolidated balance sheet	**$m**
Total stockholders' equity	17,823
Other assets (included in the above figure)	
Intangibles	1,847
Goodwill	2,385
Common stock outstanding	919.74m
Share price	$24.16

The calculations ...

Book value per share incl. intangibles (working)	$19.38 (17,823/919.74)
Book value per share excl. intangibles (working)	$14.78 (17,823 − 1,847 − 2,385)/919.74
Price to book (including intangibles) (working)	**1.25** (24.16/19.38)
Price to book (excluding intangibles) (working)	**1.63** (24.16/14.78)

Sony's accounts provide a neat illustration of some of the issues involved in calculating meaningful book value. In particular, Sony has significant intangibles and goodwill in its accounts. These relate to brand names, software titles, film and music back catalogues, and recording contracts. Many of these have real value. However, the example shows two calculations for book value, one excluding intangibles and goodwill, and one including these items.

WHAT IT MEANS

Opinions differ about how to calculate book value. Most definitions exclude minority interests (the proportion of assets in partly owned subsidiaries that is owned by outside shareholders) and goodwill.

Another issue related to definition is how to treat the value placed on property assets, and listed and unlisted investments. The most common convention is that long-term property assets can be included on the basis of an annual revaluation, that listed investments can be included at cost or market value, and unlisted investments can be included at cost. These distinctions become important when using "price to book" as a tool for comparing different companies.

In Sony's case, as explained above, intangibles are a significant element. They do not simply reflect the goodwill generated by an acquisitive company, but that of a company that has brand names, intellectual property rights, and contracts of real worth. So it is legitimate to include them as assets.

While "price to book" is a widely used quick yardstick, it needs interpreting with care, and not just because of the quirks of the calculation explained above. The more serious objection to it is that, while it works well for companies that are rich in tangible assets, it is less meaningful for those that have substantial elements of goodwill in their balance sheets.

Arguably, what matters more is not where the share price stands in relation to assets, but the profits that management generates from the assets at its disposal. Return on assets is much more relevant to the long-term value of a company as an investment. We return to this theme later in "Magic numbers" 7 and 24.

Enterprise Value to Sales

THE DEFINITION

Enterprise value (EV) is the aggregate market value of a company's listed shares, plus its debt and minus its cash. By comparing enterprise value with sales, we get a measure of value that appears to have a good record at predicting future share price performance.

THE FORMULAS

EV to sales = (market capitalization + total debt − cash)/sales

Market capitalization = issued shares × share price

THE COMPONENTS

Issued shares (common stock) outstanding – shares that have been issued and are publicly traded. See the expanded definition in the previous *Magic Numbers*.

Share (stock) price – as before, this is the current market price of the shares, normally the mid-market price at the close of business on the previous trading day.

Total debt – the total of long- and short-term debt issued or owed by the company and its subsidiaries. This could include bank loans and overdrafts, medium- and long-term loans (secured or unsecured), bonds, and all other debt of a similar type.

Cash – cash held in the company's bank account or any liquid investments that can be turned into cash instantly. These would normally include, for example, certificates of deposit (CDs) and other liquid assets, but not investments in shares or other securities whose value could fluctuate sharply from day to day.

Annual sales – sales, revenue, or turnover are virtually interchangeable terms and are in such common use as to need little further explanation. Where calculations differ is in whether or not, in performing this calculation, you take the sales for the last reported year, or the last 12 months.

WHERE'S THE DATA?

Issued shares (common stock) outstanding – in the notes to the accounts. The reference to the note in the consolidated balance sheet should be next to the heading, "called-up share capital" or a similar term. See the expanded definition in the previous *Magic Numbers*.

Share (stock) price – from any daily newspaper or financial web site. Take care to use the actual share price and not that of any options, warrants, partly paid shares, or any other derivatives.

Total debt – from the consolidated (or "group") balance sheet within the heading "accounts payable," "creditors," or "current liabilities" (for short-term debt), and further down the page for medium- and long-term loans. You may need to look at the relevant note to the accounts. The total debt figure may be the sum of two or three relevant items that must be separately identified.

Cash – from the consolidated (or "group") balance sheet, within the heading "current assets."

Annual sales – the topmost figure or subtotal in the consolidated profit and loss account or income statement.

Calculating it – the Theory

Figure 3.1 shows the different numbers to be pulled from the accounts and how to use them to calculate the ratio.

Figure 3.1 Calculating the "Magic Number" for enterprise value/sales

Widget Consolidated Industries has ...	
Market capitalization of ...	$125m
Short-term debt of ...	$25m
Long-term debt of ...	$25m
Cash of ...	$10m
Annual sales of ...	$80m
Enterprise value is ... (working)	**$165m** (125 + 25 + 25 − 10)
Enterprise value/sales is ... (working)	**2.06 times** (165/80)

CALCULATING IT FOR
ALTRIA

Figure 3.2 shows how you can use the selected numbers from the summary of Altria's 2002 accounts and calculate this "magic number." Altria is the new name for Philip Morris, a large US-based cigarette" and food group. More information on the company is available at *www.altria.com.*

Figure 3.2   Calculating EV/sales from Altria's 2002 accounts

The figures ...

Issued shares	2.039bn
Share price (at time of writing)	$33.17
Total debt	$23.32bn
Cash	$0.57bn
Sales (net revenues)	$80.41bn

The calculations ...

Market capitalization (working)	**$67.63bn** (2.039 × 33.17)
Enterprise value (working)	**$90.38bn** (67.63 + 23.32 − 0.57)
EV/sales (working)	**1.12 times** (90.38/80.41)

In Altria's case, the numbers, all in billions or billions of dollars, are comparatively easy to work with.

You can also perform this calculation part way through a year from the latest profit announcement, since earnings releases generally contain sufficient information to allow you to calculate enterprise value. If you are performing the calculation part of the way through a year, you need to find an annualized sales figure. If so, calculating the sales for the last 12 months requires you to find out the total sales for the last financial year, and to add the difference between the current period to date and the comparable period of the prior year.

However, a quick way of doing this for US companies is to look at the entry for the company in Yahoo! Finance (*http://finance.yahoo.com*), where these figures are given in an easily digestible form. Look for the figure suffixed "ttm." This stands for "trailing 12 months," and is the figure you require. Details of cash and debt must be obtained from the earnings release itself. The figure at the end of the most recent period can be taken.

WHAT IT MEANS

As we saw in "Magic number" 1, when looking at the price to sales ratio, calculations like this can be a very sound indicator of whether a share is cheap or expensive, both in absolute terms and relative to its peers.

As we noted, James O'Shaughnessy's book, *What Works on Wall Street*, contains compelling evidence that price to sales ratio (the ratio of market value to sales) has been one of the most reliable indicators of future share price performance.

EV/sales, like the PSR, is also one of the simplest ratios for any investor to calculate.

Research from Morgan Stanley in December 2002 (*European Stock Selection – the factors that matter*, p. 2) tested 25 different factors for stock selection within Europe over the previous 15 years. While many other measures were highly significant, it describes EV/sales as "the most consistent measure [for stock selection] across most sectors."

As the evidence of the past few years has shown, some companies have tried to fudge their sales figures. However, the vast majority of companies, like Altria, are honest. Sales performance remains one of the key performance indicators when it comes to measuring a company's success at doing business. Provided we take care to be skeptical about sales revenue figures where appropriate (for example, where companies are accounting for long-term contracts, or have discretion about how revenue is recognized), using sales as a basis for share valuation methods makes sense.

Using enterprise value as the numerator adds an extra dimension to market value. This is because it brings in the company's long-term capital structure as a factor in valuation. Companies with high borrowings look more expensive than those with low borrowings, or net cash in the bank. This means that companies that look cheap on this measure are likely also to be less risky for investors.

A good rule of thumb for the PSR, as we saw in the previous book, is a number less than one. This was O'Shaughnessy's guideline. It's unrealistic to expect most companies to function without any borrowings, so an EV/sales figure of less than 1.3 times is probably a reasonable indicator that a company's shares offer good long-term value.

EV/EBITDA

THE DEFINITION

EV/EBITDA is shorthand for a valuation method similar to the price-earnings ratio. It tries to gauge the value of the company by comparing one of the measures of its market value with a profit number derived from the income statement.

EV is enterprise value. We covered how to calculate it in the original *Magic Numbers* book. It is market capitalization plus debt minus cash. You can calculate market capitalization by taking the issued shares of a company and multiplying them by the stock price.

EBITDA is an acronym. It stands for earnings before interest, tax, depreciation, and amortization. It is "operating income" or "operating profit" after adding back the charges for depreciation of fixed assets and amortization of goodwill. The reason for disregarding these charges is that they do not involve an actual cash expense.

THE FORMULAS

EV/EBITDA = (market capitalization + total debt − cash)/
EBITDA

EBITDA = pre-tax profit + interest paid + depreciation + amortization

THE COMPONENTS

Enterprise value (EV) has four elements:

Issued shares (common stock) outstanding – these are shares that have been issued and are publicly traded.

Share (or stock) price – this is the current market price of the stock, normally the mid-market price at the close of business on the previous trading day.

Multiply these two together to arrive at *market capitalization*. EV is market capitalization plus total debt minus cash.

Total debt – this is the total of long- and short-term debt issued by or owed by the company and its subsidiaries.

Cash – this is cash held at the company's bank and any liquid investments that can be turned into cash instantly.

EBITDA – you can calculate this with relative ease from information in the company's accounts. Most income statements (profit and loss accounts) follow a similar pattern, with sales at the top. The cost of materials and other external inputs is subtracted from this figure to arrive at gross profit. From gross profit, various operating expenses are deducted to arrive at operating profit. But there are some charges like depreciation of fixed assets and amortization (annual write-offs) of goodwill that are book entries rather than actual payments.

EBITDA is operating profit after adding back the specific non-cash items of depreciation and amortization.

WHERE'S THE DATA?

EV COMPONENTS

Issued shares (common stock) outstanding – in the notes to the accounts. You can find the note from a reference in the consolidated balance sheet next to the heading, "called-up share capital" or a similar term. The number of ordinary shares at the end of the year should be taken.

Share (or stock) price – from any daily newspaper or financial web site. Note also that some newspapers save you the trouble of calculating market capitalization by including it in their share price pages. Market capitalization figures are also sometimes available for individual stocks at some financial web sites like Yahoo! Finance (*http://finance.yahoo.com*).

Total debt – you get this from the consolidated (or "group") balance sheet under the heading, "accounts payable", "creditors", or "current liabilities" (for short-term debt), and further down the page for medium- and long-term loans. Some companies conveniently provide a table in the notes to the accounts, giving the timing of debt repayments and the amounts involved. The total of this figure can be used as the figure for total debt.

Cash – from the consolidated (or "group") balance sheet, under the heading, "current assets."

EBITDA COMPONENTS

Operating profit – in the main part of the income statement, usually immediately above the "interest" line.

Depreciation – normally from one of the first few notes to the accounts, under the heading, "operating profit is taken after the following deductions," or "operating expenses include …". Take the depreciation charge for the year, not the figure for accumulated depreciation (this is the total for several previous years). Also, annual depreciation is usually given in the notes relating to fixed assets.

Amortization – this is sometimes included separately in the income statement if it is a sizeable figure or, alternatively, in the notes alongside depreciation.

CALCULATING IT – THE THEORY

Figure 4.1 shows the different numbers to be pulled from the accounts and how to use them to calculate the ratio.

Figure 4.1   Calculating the "Magic Number" for EV/EBITDA

Widgets de Paris SA has ...	
Market capitalization of ...	€125m
Short-term debt of ...	€25m
Long-term debt of ...	€25m
Cash of ...	€10m
so **EV (enterprise value) is ...**	**€165m**
(working)	(125 + 25 + 25 − 10)
It has operating profit of ...	€10m
... fixed asset depreciation of ...	€2m
... and goodwill amortization of ...	€2.5m
EBITDA is ...	**€14.5m**
(working)	(10 + 2 + 2.5)
EV/EBITDA is ...	**11.4**
(working)	(165/14.5)

CALCULATING IT FOR

WPP

Figure 4.2 shows how the highlighted numbers from this extract from the 2002 accounts of WPP combine to produce the "magic number".

Figure 4.2   Calculating EV/EBITDA from WPP's 2002 accounts

The figures ...

Shares in issue (Note 8)
At December 31, 2002 there were **1,157,325,640** shares in issue.
Share price (at time of writing)   £4.43

Consolidated balance sheet
Cash at bank and in hand   £689.1m
Current asset investments   £190.4m

Note 12
Schedule of debt repayments
Total debt   £1,602.2m

EV is ...   **£5,849.5m**
(working) $(1,157.3 \times 4.43) + (1,602.2 - 689.1 - 190.4)$

Market capitalization of £5,126.8m is added to net debt of £722.7m.

Consolidated profit and loss account
Operating profit   £272.5m

Consolidated cash flow statement
Depreciation   £116.6m
Goodwill amortization and impairment   £177.7m

EBITDA is ...   **£566.8m**
(working) $(272.5 + 116.6 + 177.7)$

The answer is operating profit after adding back depreciation and amortization.

The calculation ...

EV/EBITDA is ...   **10.3**
(working) $(5,849.5/566.8)$

WPP is a leading global advertising and marketing services company with brands such as JWT, Ogilvy & Mather, and Hill & Knowlton. There is more information on WPP at the company's corporate web site at *www.wpp.com*.

Working out market capitalization and EV will soon become second nature. When you use historic accounts data for the bottom half of the fraction, however, a particular problem will become apparent: the figures quickly become out of date. One alternative is to calculate EBITDA on a trailing 12 months' basis. In this particular instance with WPP, the argument does not apply. But generally it is good practice to try and seek out the latest trailing EBITDA figure for the company being investigated, and to include cash and debt figures from the latest available balance sheet when calculating EV.

Yahoo! Finance at *http://finance.yahoo.com*, and its sister sites for other countries (such as *http://finance.yahoo.co.uk*) provide these figures in an easily digestible form. For US companies it is possible to get a trailing 12 months EBITDA figure. For other countries it may be necessary to go back to the original company data and rework the calculations.

In WPP's case the EV/EBITDA is an important measurement. This is because the company operates in an international industry populated by companies with different capital structures. The measure allows you to compare international companies without worrying about distortions that may be introduced by differing corporate tax regimes, accounting policies, and capital structures.

Many professional investors use EV/EBITDA as an initial screen when looking for companies to research further. Generally, they look for a ratio of less than 10 times to indicate that a company may be a potential candidate to buy.

WHAT IT MEANS

EV/EBITDA is used as a means of comparing companies with high levels of debt or lots of cash, or those that are making losses at the net income level, but not necessarily further up the profit and loss column. As noted above, you can also use it for comparing companies in the same industry but in different countries.

EV is a way of valuing a company in the same way, irrespective of its capital structure. Excluding the impact of interest and tax, the taking of earnings before interest and tax (the EBIT in EBITDA) as the denominator of the fraction balances this up.

In other words, debt is added back on one side (in the EV calculation), and interest on debt is added back on the other (in EBITDA). Also, using a figure taken before deducting tax means that international differences in company tax rates can be ignored when comparing companies.

Is adding back charges like depreciation and amortization valid? The case is easier to make for amortization. It is usually related to amortizing goodwill, an arbitrary policy recently introduced by accountants.

Those seeking to exclude depreciation from the equation are on shakier ground. Depreciation reflects the fact that physical assets wear out and have to be replaced.

So though it is a notional charge at the time it is made, depreciation is a marker for a real cost that must be borne by the business. It mirrors a cash expense in the future, which will occur when the assets are replaced.

Whether valid or not, EV/EBITDA is now widely used. However, it needs to be treated with extreme care, especially where used to justify the stock market valuations of loss-making companies. If a company has sizeable income from partly-owned companies, an adjustment may need to be made for this too.

5

PEG Factor

THE DEFINITION

The PEG ratio, sometimes called the *PEG factor*, relates the price–earnings ratio (PER) of a share to the earning growth rate of the underlying company.

We explained how to calculate the price–earnings ratio in the original *Magic Numbers* book. The PER is the share price divided by earnings per share. The PEG factor is normally calculated on a "prospective" or forecast basis. This means you divide the PER based on forecast earnings by the expected percentage earnings per share growth. For instance, if the prospective PER were 15 times and the forecast earnings growth 20 percent, the PEG factor would be 0.75.

THE FORMULAS

PEG factor = **PER** (expressed as "times")/**E**arnings **G**rowth (expressed as a %)

Forecast PEG = **PER** (on forecast earnings)/**E**arnings **G**rowth (% change from last reported year to the current year)

THE COMPONENTS

Price–earnings ratio – this is the current share price divided by earnings per share. "Historic" PERs are the current share price divided by the latest reported earnings per share. "Prospective" PERs are the current share price divided by forecast earnings for the current financial year.

Earnings growth – this is *either* a long-term average of earnings growth in prior years, *or* the growth in the last reported financial year compared to the previous one, *or* the growth in earnings expected in the current (that is, as yet incomplete) financial year compared with the last reported full year.

The PEG calculation must pair up the appropriate PER with the comparable growth rate: historic PER with historic growth, or prospective PER with prospective growth.

WHERE'S THE DATA?

The elements required to calculate the PEG are:

Share (stock) price – from any daily newspaper or financial web site. Care should be taken to use the actual share price.

Earnings per share (last reported year or historic record) – this is in the income statement, normally toward the bottom of the page. The historic record of earnings per share figures may be in a table of financial highlights at the beginning or end of the accounts. Growth rates are the percentage changes from one year to another, or, for a span that covers more than two years, the average compound annual growth rate for the period in question.

Earnings per share (forecast) – a consensus of market estimates should be used. This can be found, especially for major companies, in commonly used statistical services like the United Kingdom's CD-REFS (which calculates PEGs for you) or at financial web sites such as Yahoo! Finance. See the appendix for the web addresses of some commonly used statistical services of this type.

CALCULATING IT – THE THEORY

Figure 5.1 shows the different numbers to be pulled from the accounts and how to use them to calculate the ratio.

Figure 5.1   Calculating the "Magic Number" for the PEG factor

Tokyo Widgets Corporation has ...

Financial years ending December	Reported 2001	Reported 2002	Forecast 2003
Earnings per share for these years are ...	¥22	¥25	¥35
Earnings per share growth is therefore ... (working)	–	14% ((25 × 100/22) − 100)	40% ((35 × 100/25) − 100)
The share price is ...		¥600	
Price–earnings ratio (PER) is ... (working)		**24.0** (600/25)	**17.1** (600/35)
PEG factor (based on historic PER and growth) is: (working)		**1.71** (24/14)	
PEG factor (based on forecast PER and growth) is: (working)			**0.43** (17.1/40)

CALCULATING IT FOR
STATOIL

Figure 5.2 shows how the highlighted numbers from this extract from the accounts of Statoil combine to produce the "magic number." There is more information at *www.statoil.com*. Statoil is the recently privatized and listed Norwegian former state oil company.

Figure 5.2 Calculating the PEG from Statoil's 2002 accounts

We can format this calculation in almost exactly the same way as we have done on the theoretical example in Figure 5.1, changing only the numbers and currencies.

The figures ...

Financial years ending December	Reported 2001	Reported 2002	Forecast 2003
Earnings per share (in NOK) are ...	7.14	7.56	5.63
Earnings per share growth is therefore ... (working)		5.9% ((7.56 × 100/7.14) − 100)	−25.5% ((5.63 × 100/7.56) − 100)
The share price (in NOK) is ...		55.5	

The calculations ...

Price–earnings ratio (PER) is ... (working)		7.3 (55.5/7.56)	9.9 (55.5/5.63)
PEG factor (based on historic PER and growth) is: (working)		1.24 (7.3/5.9)	
PEG factor (based on forecast PER and growth) is:			nm

The prospective PEG is not meaningful because there is no forecast growth expected.

One major problem with PEGs relates to the passage of time.

A prospective PEG taken at the beginning of the financial year contains forecast earnings figures that will not be proved right or wrong for perhaps another 12 months.

This clearly has a different validity to a PEG taken near the end of the financial year. In this case, the results for that year will be announced in a matter of weeks. Usually, by this time the consensus forecast has already been adjusted to reflect information that has emerged in the course of the year.

Comparing the PEGs on companies with different year-ends is particularly difficult because of this factor. One solution is to use a PEG calculated only on already-reported earnings growth.

There are two alternatives. Either use an up-to-the-minute calculation of earnings and earnings growth, adding up the last two half-years or last four reported quarters to make the figures as current as possible. Or use a long-term annual average of earnings growth calculated from the figures for, say, the previous five years.

However, there is a big objection to using historic figures. PEGs are really only useful for working out the right price to pay for *expected* growth.

Jim Slater, the British investment guru who invented the idea of the PEG, suggests the best way to solve this problem. It is to take the average earnings expected for the two following forecast years, weighting the calculation one way or other, depending on when in the year it is done, and then work out earnings growth and PER and PEG based on these figures.

There is no simple way around this problem, although Slater's book *Investment Made Easy* explains his concept in more detail.

The Statoil example also highlights another drawback of the PEG. While we can calculate the PEG for the company based on historic earnings, according to the consensus forecast published on the financial web site OnVista (*www.onvista.co.uk*), Statoil's earnings are expected to decline in 2003. As there is no growth expected, calculating the PEG is therefore impossible. A negative PEG is meaningless.

WHAT IT MEANS

In general, PEGs are a guide as to whether or not what you are paying for growth is reasonable. Slater's original yardstick was that the PER should be less than the earnings growth number. In other words, with a PEG of less than one, a stock starts to look cheap. The lower the number, the cheaper it gets.

This has an elegant simplicity that cannot be faulted, even though one might argue about how to deal with time differences. Interpreting PEGs, like many other "magic numbers," is often "refined" to justify excessive market valuations. Our view is that this is mistaken. If profits growth is absent, or slow, then a low multiple of those profits is all that can be justified.

PEGs only work with certain types of company. If a company is currently making losses, or its profits are falling (as in the Statoil example), or it is habitually valued on the basis of its assets or by some other measure, then the PEG will be of little or no use. It works best when comparing growth companies.

Price to Research Ratio

THE DEFINITION

This ratio compares the company's market value with the amount it spends on research and development (R&D) to try and gauge whether the stock market is putting a high or low value on this spending.

THE FORMULA

PRR = share price/R&D expenditure per share

THE COMPONENTS

R&D expenditure – this term is somewhat ambiguous. Its scope differs from company to company and industry to industry. It will range from pure research on the one hand to technology licensing, and the purchase of proprietary technology from third parties. It may even include test marketing or market research, or the cost of getting science-based products through the regulatory hurdles they may need to satisfy. There may be differences from company to company in what is and what is not included. Most companies in the same industry will probably use broadly similar conventions in the way they define this item.

Issued shares (common stock) outstanding – these are shares that have been issued and which are publicly traded. This includes shares that are "tightly held" by directors and their families, even though these may rarely change hands.

Sometimes earnings per share calculations are based on "fully diluted" issued shares outstanding. This takes in, for example, any extra shares that may be issued in the future as a result of the exercise of executive share options and other effects. If this item is significant, it is probably also worth applying this fully diluted calculation to work out R&D spending per share.

Earnings per share calculations also normally use "weighted average" shares in issue. This is the average number of shares in issue during the period when the profit was being earned, giving due weight to new shares issued during the period, in accordance with the time they were issued. New shares issued at the beginning of the year carry more weight than those issued at the end.

To be strictly accurate, calculations of R&D spending per share should work on the same weighted basis, since the spending accrues during the course of the year.

Share (stock) price – the current market price of the shares. This is normally the mid-market price at the close of business on the previous trading day.

WHERE'S THE DATA?

R&D expenditure – this is normally either disclosed on the face of the profit and loss account (income statement) or in the relevant notes to the accounts. It may be part of the note that itemizes the amounts deducted to arrive at operating profit. Most companies for which it is important will generally disclose it openly, making it easy to locate the correct figure.

Issued shares (common stock) outstanding – weighted average shares in issue during the year can usually be found in the note to the accounts referring to the earnings per share calculation.

Share (stock) price – from any daily newspaper or financial web site. Take care to use the actual share price and not the prices of any options, warrants, partly paid shares, or other derivatives. Take note also of the units in which the share price is expressed. In the United Kingdom, shares are traditionally quoted in pence, but in dollars in the United States and in Continental Europe. You need to make sure that the R&D spending per-share figure conforms to the same units as the price, so that you are comparing like with like.

CALCULATING IT – THE THEORY

Figure 6.1 shows a fictional example of how the highlighted numbers can be used to calculate the ratios in question.

Figure 6.1   Calculating the "Magic Number" for price to research ratio

Widget BioPharma has the following profit and loss account numbers and share price data:

Year to 31 December (Singapore $m)	2002	2001
Revenue	250	200
less		
Cost of sales	100	98
R&D expenditure	35	34
Selling, general, and administrative	65	50
Operating profit	50	18
Weighted average shares in issue (m)	70	65
Current share price	4.00	
R&D expenditure per share is ...	$0.50	$0.52
(working)	(35/70)	(34/65)
PRR is ...	8.0	7.7
(working)	(4.00/0.5)	(4.00/0.52)

CALCULATING IT FOR
MICROSOFT, GSK, AND SONY

Figure 6.2 shows how the highlighted numbers from the extracts of the accounts of Microsoft, GlaxoSmithKline, and Sony combine to produce the "magic numbers."

Figure 6.2   Calculating it for Microsoft, GSK, and Sony

The figures ...

	Microsoft Jun-02 $m	GSK Dec-02 £m	Sony Mar-02 ¥bn
Extract from income statement, year to:			
Revenue, sales, or turnover	28,365	21,212	7,578
R&D expenditure	4,307	2,900	433.2
Weighted average shares in issue (m)	11,106.0	5,934.0	919.7
Current share price May 19, 2003	$24.80	£12.51	¥2,930

The calculations ...

	Microsoft	GSK	Sony
R&D per share is ...	$0.39	£0.49	¥471
(working)	(4,307/11,106)	(2,900/5,934)	(433,200/919.7)

All figures converted to millions for the purposes of calculation.

	Microsoft	GSK	Sony
PRR is ... (times)	63.6	25.5	6.2
(working)	(24.80/0.39)	(12.51/0.49)	(2,930/471)

This calculation is fairly straightforward. We have taken fully diluted shares in issue where appropriate to calculate the R&D per-share figure. We could, however, perform the calculation another way. We could work out the company's stock market capitalization and then compare this with the R&D number straight from the accounts. However, since market capitalization calculations traditionally use the latest available shares in issue figure, this would often produce a slightly different result.

What it Means

The results of the example point up one reason why this calculation is valuable and one of its drawbacks.

In theory there is no reason why we can't compare companies in this way across borders. It is sometimes suggested that the greater percentage of sales a company spends on R&D, the more highly the market is likely to value that spending. In fact, though we haven't calculated it here, Microsoft spends three times as much as Sony in terms of R&D as a percentage of sales. Microsoft's PRR is approximately 10 times that of Sony.

One reason for this is undoubtedly the sharp difference in the general level of stock market values in the United States as opposed to Japan. Despite the sharp fall in Microsoft's share price over the past couple of years, we need to bear in mind that Japanese equities have been in a bear market for more than a decade.

But the market may in fact be behaving rationally. Sony's return on equity and margins are less than Microsoft's. The market may simply be making the judgement that, based on its past record, Microsoft will ultimately generate more sales, profits, and cash from its R&D spending than Sony is likely to. If so, it makes sense that its spending should be valued more highly as a result.

It is, however, probably more appropriate to use this number when we are comparing companies in the same industry and the same country. Some observers believe it is a particularly useful ratio to use when companies are research intensive and are therefore making losses when measured by conventional accounting.

Analysts would then use a combination of price to sales and price to research ratios to try and work out which company had the most future potential. It would also be relevant in this context to use the "burn rate" calculation we explored in the original *Magic Numbers* book to decide how long the company might be able to survive on its present cash resources without further fundraising. Software companies and biotech and other science-based businesses are obvious examples where analysis techniques like this can be used.

Reinvested Return on Equity

THE DEFINITION

Reinvested return on equity attempts to project forward the future value of a company and its shares. It then relates this to the price that investors must pay today to buy the shares. It rests on several key concepts, including the company's return on equity, dividend payout and retention ratio, and the market's risk-free rate of return.

We covered all of these concepts in some detail in the original *Magic Numbers*. I will, however, just recap them before we go further.

Return on equity (ROE) is a measure of how efficient a company's management is at deploying the equity in the company that is collectively owned by all the shareholders. The *payout ratio* is the percentage of earnings per share paid out in dividends. The *retention ratio* is the percentage of earnings per share not paid out in dividends, but retained for reinvestment. The market's *risk-free rate of return* is the return you could get investing your cash in a risk-free government bond.

The idea is that if a company has a high return on equity, the more of that return it keeps reinvesting the better. This is because the profits earned, but retained in the company, will almost certainly cause a higher return to be ploughed back into the business than if they landed in your pocket and were invested elsewhere or spent.

Say a company whose shares you hold has an ROE of 20 percent, but pays out half its profits in dividends. To be better off on balance, you have to try and replicate that 20 percent by investing the dividend elsewhere. It may be difficult. We all tend to overestimate our stock-picking ability. A proven growth stock generating high returns can be one of the best long-term homes for your money.

By looking at reinvested ROE we can show how this compounding works for any given level of ROE, dividend payout, and risk-free rate of return. It is a way of getting down to the crux of long-term share valuation and how it can work for you.

The Formula

The formula is most suitable for a spreadsheet application. The reinvested ROE spreadsheet can be downloaded from *www. magicnumbersbook.com.*

It works like this. Return on average equity is calculated and adjusted to reflect the proportion of profits retained. Then the model calculates a "year 5" value for the company, based on profits implied from the growth generated in shareholders' equity.

A market multiple is then applied to year 5 profits to arrive at the year 5 company value. After factoring in the value of dividends over the period, this is compared with the current market capitalization. A compound rate of return is calculated that equates the two. For a sufficient margin of safety to be present in the investment, this return should probably be at least 20 percent per annum.

The Components

Return on equity – after-tax profits expressed as a percentage of average shareholders' funds (including any accumulated goodwill). Calculating return on equity is a simple matter of taking net income and expressing it as a percentage of the average of the last two years' stockholders' equity, including cumulative goodwill.

We include cumulative goodwill, whether or not it has been written off, for a reason. This is because, whether it is written off or not, it is shareholders' capital that has been spent by management in the past. Whether the spending was wise or not it should not be ignored.

Calculated in this way, a company's percentage return on equity is an important measure of its ability to continue to produce high returns in the future.

The higher the return and the higher the percentage retained for reinvestment, the more cash is put to work to continue earning these returns in the future. This should mean that the intrinsic value of the company in the future is enhanced.

Retention rate – this is calculated by subtracting dividends from after-tax profit and dividing by after-tax profits. If a company has profits of 10p a share and pays 2.5p out in dividends, it is retaining 7.5p (10.0 − 2.5), and its retention rate is therefore 75 percent (7.5/10.0).

Capitalization rate – the capitalization rate is the rate used to multiply up year 5 projected profits to get to the projected company value in that year. The rate can be established from some form of benchmark yield (the capitalization rate would simply be the reciprocal of the yield), or else it can be chosen on some other basis, perhaps the company's current earnings multiple, a sector multiple, or a long-term average market multiple.

If a yield-based yardstick is used, the obvious choice is to use the reciprocal of the risk-free rate of return on a government bond maturing in, say, five years. More conservatively, you could use the reciprocal of the risk-free rate plus an "equity risk premium" of, say, 4 percent. Say the risk-free rate is 3.5 percent and the equity risk premium is 4 percent, the options would be to use a multiple of 26.6 (the reciprocal of 3.5%), which you may consider excessive relative to the market's long-term average multiple. Or you could use a multiple of 13.3 (the reciprocal of 7.5%), which reflects the equity risk premium and is more justifiable.

WHERE'S THE DATA?

Net income – this is toward the bottom of the income statement. In UK parlance this is net profit attributable to shareholders.

Shareholders' funds (stockholders' equity) – this is in the consolidated balance sheet, usually at the bottom right-hand corner of a double page. The figure is the total of all assets, including intangible assets and goodwill, minus all liabilities and provisions. The residual is what is "owned" by stockholders. If goodwill is not included here, it should be identified in the notes to the accounts (usually in a note relating to fixed assets) and added back. Cumulative goodwill, rather than the charge for a particular year, is the correct figure to take. In order to get the correct average for stockholders' equity, it is necessary to perform this goodwill adjustment in both the latest year and the prior one.

Retention ratio – this can be calculated by taking the dividend per share (dps) and earnings per share (eps) figures from the bottom of the income statement, or from the summary of the company's record and applying the formula (earnings per share − dividend per share × 100)/eps. If a company pays no dividend the retention ratio is 100 percent.

Risk-free rate of return − take the redemption yield on a typical five-year government bond from your financial newspaper. Add a notional risk premium if you feel it is appropriate. The *capitalization rate* for profits is simply the reciprocal of this yield (risk-free rate, or risk-free rate plus the equity risk premium).

CALCULATING IT − THE THEORY

Valuing companies using reinvested return on equity is an easy idea to grasp and is susceptible to spreadsheet analysis. A spreadsheet that lets you perform this calculation easily is available for download at *www.magicnumbersbook.com*.

With this, you can extract a few figures from a company's report and accounts, make a small judgement here and there, and use the spreadsheet to produce a sound guide as to whether a company's shares are good value or not.

Figure 7.1 shows the different numbers to be pulled from the accounts and how to use them in the spreadsheet.

The items in italic are those that need to be calculated by the user. All other items are calculated automatically.

Figure 7.1 Calculating the "Magic Number" for reinvested ROE

Consolidated Flanges has various relevant balance sheet and income statement parameters as shown below.

Latest year-end	**Dec-02***	
Hist. shareholders' funds (£m)	110.00*	
Avg. shareholders' funds (£m)	100.00*	
Hist. after-tax profit (£m)	25.00*	
Historic dividends (£m)	6.50*	
Average ROE (%)	25.00	
Retention rate	0.74	
Reinvestment ROE (%)	18.50	
Shareholders ... (£m)	**Equity**	**Dividends**
Future year 1	130.35	8.47
Future year 2	154.46	10.04
Future year 3	183.04	11.90
Future year 4	216.90	14.10
Future year 5	257.03	16.71
Total		**61.22**
Future year 5 after-tax profit (£m)	**64.26**	
Benchmark yield (%)	3.95*	
Implied multiple	25.32	
Capitalized year 5 PAT (£m)	1,626.77	
Total return incl. divs (£m)	1,687.99	
Current mkt cap. (£m)	450.00*	
% uplift/"margin of safety"	275.11*	
Implied % compound return	30.3%*	

Figures marked with an asterisk are those required to be entered or calculated by the user. The rest are calculated automatically.

To recap on why the figure looks as it does:

First, the worksheet calculates average return on equity (ROE). This calculation divides after-tax profit by average shareholder's funds, and expresses the result as a percentage.

The model works out the retention rate. It is the percentage of profits left over after dividends have been paid.

The reinvestment rate of return is calculated by multiplying ROE by the retention rate.

Shareholders' equity and after-tax profits are then compounded at this rate for five years. Dividends are assumed to rise in proportion from year 1 onwards.

The year 5 after-tax profit is calculated either by "grossing up" the dividend in "future year 5" by the retention rate, or by applying the historic ROE figure to the year 5 shareholders' equity figure. The result is the same either way.

The year 5 after-tax profit is then multiplied by the capitalization rate, and the resulting figure added to accumulated dividends to arrive at a year 5 value for the company.

This is compared with the current market capitalization to establish the percentage annual return required to equate one to the other. This figure, represented by the potential uplift from the current market value to the project value of the company five years from now, demonstrates the long-term cheapness (or lack of it) implied by the current market price of the shares.

The implied rate of return can be calculated either from compound interest tables or by using a financial calculator.

As can be seen, in this case, the result is a projected rate of return of 30 percent. This would justify investing in the company.

CALCULATING IT FOR

McDONALD'S

Figure 7.2 shows how the highlighted numbers from this extract from the accounts of McDonald's combine to produce the "magic number." McDonald's is a US-based global fast food restaurant chain operating through both company-owned and franchised outlets. More information on the company can be had from *www.mcdonalds.com*.

Figure 7.2 Calculating reinvested return on equity from McDonald's 2002 accounts

McDonald's has various relevant balance sheet and income statement parameters as shown below.

Latest year-end	Dec-02*	
Hist. shareholders' funds ($m)	10,281.00*	
Avg. shareholders' funds ($m)	9,488.40*	
Hist. after-tax profit ($m)	992.10*	
Historic dividends ($m)	309.20*	
Average ROE (%)	10.46	
Retention rate	0.69	
Reinvestment ROE (%)	7.20	
Shareholders ... ($m)	**Equity**	**Dividends**
Future year 1	11,020.95	359.14
Future year 2	11,814.15	384.99
Future year 3	12,664.43	412.70
Future year 4	13,575.92	442.40
Future year 5	14,553.01	474.24
Total		**2,073.47**
Future year 5 after-tax profit ($m)	**1,521.65**	
Benchmark yield (%)	3.07*	
Implied multiple	32.57	
Capitalized year 5 PAT ($m)	49,565.20	
Total return incl. divs ($m)	51,638.67	
Current mkt cap. ($m)	21,793.20*	
% uplift/"margin of safety"	136.95*	
Implied % compound return	18.8%*	

Figures marked with an asterisk are those required to be entered or calculated by the user. The rest are calculated automatically.

McDonald's faced a torrid time in 2002 with declining profits and a slumping share price. However, the calculation cuts through this emotional background to look at the company on the basis of objective market-tested numbers. Note in particular that McDonald's cumulative goodwill is carried on the face of the balance sheet, so there is no need to hunt in the notes to make adjustments.

The company's problem is clear: a relatively low reinvestment return on equity. Even with the help of a relatively low five-year Treasury bond yield and therefore the ability to capitalize year 5 profits by a hefty multiple, the depressed current share price suggests that the shares might be worth a little more than double their current price in five year's time. This could mean they are cheap. Investors have to expect returns to be relatively modest in the future. An 18.8 percent projected annual compound return from a company as pervasive as McDonald's could be construed as attractive.

What it Means

There are advantages to an approach like this. The "magic number" is comparatively simple to calculate using a spreadsheet. It also gives due weight to the importance of return on equity in generating value for shareholders, which many other methods of valuing shares don't. It rewards those companies that retain a high proportion of their profits for reinvestment in the business. And it allows market-tested yields to be incorporated into the valuation, rather than a more random variable.

There are, however, also some drawbacks. It works well only with those companies that have relatively straightforward balance sheets and a steadily growing business. Asset-based or income-orientated investments do not fit well with this approach, but can nonetheless be legitimate investment choices.

Part Two

Income Statement "Magic Numbers"

INCOME STATEMENT "MAGIC NUMBERS"

The seven ratios included in this section are derived from the profit and loss account, or income statement. With the exception of margins, none was included in the original edition of *Magic Numbers*. All of the examples are new.

The ratios allow you get a more in-depth view of the sales performance and cost structure of the business, and how they affect profitability and returns to shareholders. This section has several permutations on the way investors can view these numbers.

Income statement magic numbers reflect the quality of the earnings figures and the underlying long-term strength of the business, rather than the immediate valuation the market is placing on it.

- Sales, earnings, and shareholders' equity each have a key bearing on understanding the company's business and how it functions on a daily basis. Here we look at them in per-share terms. Each can also be expressed in terms of the other to get a fuller understanding of how they interact and what they tell you about a company's earning power.

- Staff are an important part of any business. It is important that their costs are kept within bounds. You can measure this by looking at staff costs as a percentage of sales, and more pointedly by looking at management remuneration in a similar way, too. You can also look at sales and profit per employee to measure the trends in the productivity the company is achieving from its staff.

- Much has been written in the press about "pro-forma" earnings. They serve a purpose when used correctly. However, the technique has more commonly been used recently to present an unduly rosy view of a company's profitability. Distinguishing between these two uses of the term is vital.

- Finally, there are margins. These are important measures of company profitability and can be struck at various points down the income statement column. They are key pointers to a company's efficiency at controlling costs and, as they change over time, indicators of the intensity of external competitive pressures.

Interpreting the numbers is as important as knowing how to calculate them. Often the process is less straightforward than it might seem.

For most of the numbers contained in this section, it is important to look at the trend in the ratio over a period of years. Use a five-year run of numbers where possible. If you do, trends can be spotted and years when aberrations occur can be identified and excluded.

Staff costs should be looked at in this way, too. But in many cases it is hard to consider them just in this way. Staff costs as a percentage of sales are only one dimension of the staff cost equation. They need to be looked at in terms of average employee remuneration, and in profit and sales per employee. The numbers are more important for some businesses than for others. And they assume more importance for individual businesses at different times in the business cycle. You need to judge the significance of the ratio in question for the type of business you are investigating.

The level of management remuneration is a complex topic, and one that is perennially topical. For companies in the top tier of the stock market, or those in the same industry, comparing management remuneration relative to profits is a measure of the value shareholders are getting out of the company's officers and directors.

"Pro-forma" earnings are a legitimate form of analysis when used to give a more meaningful picture of a company's accounts. The classic use of this technique used to be to adjust for a takeover part way through the year. The pro-forma calculation produced figures based on what they would have been as if the acquired company had been owned for a full 12 months. This useful technique has, however, been dragged into disrepute. Read on to find out how.

Interpreting margins is fairly easy, but the calculation needs to be done carefully, to make sure the figures are truly comparable with prior years at the same company and across the company's peer group.

As in other sections of this book, the pages that follow examine each of these seven "magic numbers" in more depth.

As usual, we have used real-life examples and extracts from the actual accounts of companies in different parts of the world to demonstrate the calculations in practice.

Let us also repeat our warning from the original book. Remember that the income statement is the least reliable part of a company's accounts, and the one where management has the most leeway to manipulate the figures. Keep your eyes open for inconsistencies. If the figures look too good to be true, they probably are!

8 Sales, Earnings, and Equity Per Share

THE DEFINITION

The *sales per share ratio* is the company's annual sales (sometimes called turnover) divided by the average number of shares in issue during the year in question.

Earnings per share are the company's net income divided by the average number of shares in issue during the year in question.

Equity per share is the net assets attributable to ordinary shareholders (sometimes called book value or stockholders' equity) divided by the number of shares in issue at the end of the year in question.

THE FORMULAS

Sales per share = annual sales/average shares in issue

Earnings per share = annual net income/average shares in issue

Equity per share = year-end shareholders' equity/year-end shares in issue

THE COMPONENTS

Annual sales – sales, revenue, or turnover are virtually interchangeable terms. They are in such common use as to need little further explanation. Where calculations sometimes differ is in whether or not, in performing this calculation, you take the sales for the last reported year, or the last 12 months. In this particular set of ratios it is important that sales per share, earnings per share, and equity per share all relate to the same 12-month period and period-end. In practice, this means taking year-end numbers for all three items.

Net income – this is profit attributable to shareholders after deducting tax and minority interests. Minority interests are the profits that are "owned" by other shareholders in subsidiaries that are less than 100 percent owned.

Shareholders' equity – this goes by a number of different names, including stockholders' equity, book value, shareholders' funds, net assets, net tangible assets, and so on. Take the tangible fixed assets of the business plus current assets, and subtract current liabilities, long-term creditors, and provisions. The balance represents the residual assets that are "owned" by shareholders.

Issued shares (common stock) outstanding – these are shares that have been issued and are publicly traded. This includes shares that are "tightly held" by directors and their families, even though these may rarely change hands.

Sometimes earnings per share calculations are based on "fully diluted" issued shares outstanding. This takes in, for example, any extra shares that may be issued in the future as a result of the exercise of executive share options and other effects.

Sales and earnings per share calculations normally use "weighted average" shares in issue. This is the average number of shares in issue during the period. It gives due weight to new shares issued during the period, in accordance with the time they were issued. New shares issued at the beginning of the year carry more weight than those issued at the end.

By contrast, shareholders' equity or book value per share calculations use shares in issue at the year-end as the denominator. This is because balance sheet figures are always taken as a snapshot at the year-end.

For sales and earnings figures, which accrue over the course of the year, average shares in issue during the year are more meaningful to use when calculating per-share figures.

WHERE'S THE DATA?

Annual sales – normally the topmost figure or subtotal in the consolidated profit and loss account or income statement. Any sales deriving from large one-off business disposals may distort the figure and should, if appropriate, be excluded.

Net income – this is found in the profit and loss account (income statement), normally at the bottom of the page. Profit earned for ordinary shareholders (stockholders) should be used. This is the profit figure before any ordinary dividend payments are deducted.

Shareholders' equity – this is on the face of the consolidated balance sheet, normally identified using one of the alternative phrases listed earlier. It is also the total of share capital and reserves. Purists also add back to this figure the cumulative goodwill written off, since this represents capital that has been deployed by management on behalf of shareholders. If the figure is material, it may be appropriate to do so in this case. See "Magic number" 7 for reinvested return on equity for a more detailed explanation of the case for doing this.

Issued shares outstanding – these are in the notes to the accounts. You can find the note from a reference in the consolidated balance sheet next to the heading, "called-up share capital" or a similar term. Take the number of ordinary shares at the end of the year, not their stated nominal money value (if any).

Weighted average shares in issue during the year can usually be found in the note to the accounts referring to the earnings per share calculation.

CALCULATING IT – THE THEORY

Figure 8.1 shows the different numbers to be pulled from the accounts and how to use them to calculate these ratios.

Figure 8.1   Calculating the "Magic Numbers" for sales, earnings, and equity per share

WidgetIndustries.com Inc. has balance sheet and income statement numbers that include the following:

Sales	$100m
Net income	$15m
Shareholders' equity	$70m
Weighted average shares in issue	80m
Year-end shares in issue	85m
Sales per share is ... (working)	**$1.25** (100/80)
Earnings per share is ... (working)	**18.75 cents** (15/80)
Equity per share is ... (working)	**82.35 cents** (70/85)

CALCULATING IT FOR
HUTCHISON WHAMPOA

Figure 8.2 shows how the highlighted numbers from the accounts of Hutchison Whampoa combine to produce the figures for sales, earnings, and equity per share. Hutchison is a Hong Kong-based international trading company. It has interests in ports, property and hotels, telecoms, retail, and energy. The company's web site (*www.hutchison-whampoa.com*) has more information on the group's operations.

Figure 8.2   Calculating sales, earnings, and equity per share from Hutchison Whampoa's' 2002 accounts

The figures (in HK$, except per share amounts) ...

Consolidated profit & loss account:

Year to December 31	2002	2001*
Turnover	**111,129**	**89,038**
Profit before tax	18,878	16,203
Taxation	−2,724	−2,305
Profit after tax	16,154	13,898
Minority interests	−1,866	−1,810
Profit attributable to shareholders	**14,288**	**12,088**

Consolidated balance sheet as at December 31	2002	2001*
Capital and reserves		
Share capital	1,066	1,066
Reserves	225,110	217,207
Equity shareholders' funds	**226,176**	**218,273**

Note 12 Earnings per share

The calculation of earnings per share is based on **4,263,370,780** shares in issue during 2002 (2001 − 4,263,370,780)

*As reported, without reflecting subsequent restatements.

The calculations ...

Sales per share	**HK$26.07**	**HK$20.89**
(working – figures in millions)	(111,129/4,263)	(89,038/4,263)
Earnings per share	**HK$3.35**	**HK$2.84**
(working – figures in millions)	(14,288/4,263)	(12,088/4,263)
Equity per share	**HK$53.06**	**HK$51.20**
(working – figures in millions)	(226,176/4,263)	(218,273/4,263)

The relevant figures are converted into millions to aid comparison and then rounded where necessary. Note that because shares in issue have not changed from one year to the next, weighted average and year-end shares in issue are the same number.

WHAT IT MEANS

What really matters (or should matter) to shareholders is the size of the claim over sales, profits, and assets that each share they own represents.

Companies use shares as currency for acquisitions and, via share options, to remunerate employees and directors. These days, too, it has become accepted practice for companies to use their cash to buy back their shares for cancellation.

Why express sales, earnings, and assets as per-share numbers? One reason is that you can gauge more easily to what extent any increase in, for example, sales has been because of sales added as a result of acquisitions for shares. Alternatively, growth in earnings per share may be good, but this could be because a lackluster pattern of underlying profits has been flattered, when viewed at the per-share level, by share buybacks.

In other words has growth in sales or earnings been simply bought or engineered?

Investors rightly prefer growth that is "organic" (that is, internally generated), rather than simply the result of artificial financial transactions that may not be capable of repetition.

To put these per-share figures in context, you also need to work out the same figure for a series of years. A five-year history is a good run of numbers to aim at. Many companies provide a summary of their historic record in their published accounts. By comparing the nominal sales, earnings, and equity figures with their per-share equivalents, it should be possible to observe the degree to which the changes seen in the nominal figures might have been affected by movements in the numbers of shares in issue.

Always bear in mind, too, that companies will tend to give prominence to the per-share figures that show their record in the best light. Given the choice, I would prefer to see a figure that reflects all the potential issues of shares that might come about as a result of the exercise of share options, or conversion of convertible bonds, even if they may only be issued at some time in the future. By the same token, I don't want to see costs and charges removed arbitrarily just to make things look better.

In the example of Hutchison Whampoa, however, this question does not arise. Shares in issue have not changed from one year to the next, making the calculations comparatively simple to perform. We have no need to identify year-end shares in issue separately because there has been no change in the company's share capital from one year to the next. Because of this, it follows that year-end and weighted average shares in issue must be one and the same.

One other use of per-share figures for sales earnings and equity (or book value) is that it allows for easy comparison with the share price. Price to sales ratios and price to book value can, for example, be calculated with ease, as can the humble PER. Calculating all of these ratios from first principles was included in the original *Magic Numbers* book and is also shown in this book in the previous section.

9 Sales, Earnings, and Equity Per Share Ratios

THE DEFINITION

Each of the figures derived in "Magic number" 8 can be divided into the other to produce a set of ratios that tells us meaningful things about a company's performance.

The simplest way of expressing these is as a figure "per £ (or $, or €) of" another. We can look at sales per £ (or $, or €) of equity, earnings per £ (or $, or €) of sales, and earnings per £ (or $, or €) of sales.

THE FORMULAS

Sales per £ of equity = sales per share/average equity per share

Earnings per £ of sales = earnings per share/sales per share

Earnings per £ of equity = earnings per share/average equity per share

THE COMPONENTS

The components involved in calculating these numbers are the same as those used in the preceding "magic number." To recap in brief:

Annual sales – sales, revenue, or turnover are virtually inter-changeable terms. They are in such common use as to need little further explanation. Where calculations differ is in whether or not, in performing this calculation, you take the sales for the last reported year, or the last 12 months.

Net income – the profit attributable to shareholders after tax.

Shareholders' equity – also called stockholders' equity, book value, shareholders' funds, net assets, net tangible assets, and so on. The item comprises the tangible (and sometimes intangible) fixed assets of the business plus current assets, but minus current liabilities, long-term creditors, and provisions. In all, these are the residual assets that are "owned" by shareholders.

Issued shares (common stock) outstanding – these are shares that are issued and are publicly traded. Use weighted average shares for earnings and sales-per-share calculations and year-end shares in issue for the equity-per-share calculation.

WHERE'S THE DATA?

You can find the data used to calculate these different components and ratios that are in turn derived from them in the places mentioned in the preceding "magic number." Again to recap in brief:

Annual sales – the topmost figure or subtotal in the consolidated profit and loss account or income statement.

Net income – this is found in the profit and loss account (income statement), normally at the bottom of the page. Profit earned for ordinary shareholders (stockholders) should be used.

Shareholders' equity – this is on the face of the consolidated balance sheet. It is often identifiable as the total of share capital and reserves. You may wish to add back cumulative goodwill written off (found in the fixed-asset note), if material.

Issued shares outstanding – this item is in the notes to the accounts. The note can be found from a reference in the consolidated balance sheet next to the heading, "called-up share capital" or a similar term. The number of ordinary shares at the end of the year should be taken when calculating equity per share, and not their stated nominal money value.

Weighted average shares in issue during the year are usually in the note to the accounts referring to the earnings-per-share calculation. These are used to calculate sales and earnings per share.

CALCULATING IT – THE THEORY

Continuing on in logical steps from the numbers given in the example in Figure 8.1, these ratios can be calculated as illustrated in Figure 9.1.

Figure 9.1   Calculating the "Magic Numbers" for sales, earnings, and equity per share ratios

WidgetIndustries.com Inc. has balance sheet and income statement numbers that include the following:

	2002 $m	2001 $m
Sales	100	90
Net income	15	12
Shareholders' equity	70	65
Weighted average shares in issue	80m	80m
Year-end shares in issue	85m	80m
Sales per share is ...	**$1.25**	
(working)	(100/80)	
Earnings per share is ...	**18.75 cents**	
(working)	(15/80)	
Equity per share is ...	**82.35 cents**	**81.25 cents**
(working)	(70/85)	(65/80)

Following on from this ...

Sales per $ of average equity is ...	**$1.53**
(working)	(1.25/((0.8235 + 0.8125)/2)

Sales per share of $1.25 is divided by 0.818 – the average of 82.35 cents and 81.25 cents

Earnings per $ of sales is ...	**15 cents**
(working)	(0.1875/1.25)
Earnings per $ of average equity is ...	**22.9 cents**
(working)	(0.1875/0.818)

Earnings per share are divided by the average equity figure calculated earlier.

CALCULATING IT FOR
HUTCHISON WHAMPOA

Figure 9.2 shows how the highlighted numbers derived from the accounts of Hutchison Whampoa in Figure 8.2 combine to produce the ratios of sales per $ of equity, and earnings per $ of sales and per $ of equity.

Figure 9.2   Calculating sales, earnings, and equity per share ratios from Hutchison Whampoa's 2002 accounts

	2002 (HK$)	2001 (HK$)
The figures (from the result of Figure 8.2) ...		
Sales per share	26.07	
Earnings per share	3.35	
Equity per share	53.06	51.20
The calculations ...		
Sales per $ of equity is ...	**HK$0.50**	
(working)	(26.07/((51.20 + 53.06)/2))	
Equates to 26.07 divided by 52.13, the average of 51.20 and 53.06.		
Earnings per $ of sales is ...	**HK$0.129**	
(working)	(3.35/26.07)	
Earnings per $ of average equity is ...	**HK$0.0643**	
(working)	(3.35/52.13)	
Average equity is HK$52.13 as previously calculated.		

WHAT IT MEANS

Two out of the three ratios are another way of expressing some of the "magic numbers" that were described in the original book. Earnings per £ (or in this case per HK$) of average equity is an alternate description for return on average equity ("Magic number" 20 in the original book), while earnings per £ of sales is another way of expressing net profit margin (included in "Magic number" 9 in the original book).

Let's start, however, with sales per £ of average equity. In effect, this figure helps to tell you how good a company management team is at using the capital provided by shareholders to generate sales revenue. However, remember that sales are not the be all and end all. Sales figures can be manipulated in various ways. What ultimately matters in a business is the conversion of sales invoices into cash in the bank.

Earnings per £ (or HK$) of sales is a measure of the amount of profit generated by each £ in sales. Once again, profits can be manipulated, but as a general rule profits will mean that cash has been created. Both measures can be combined – management uses shareholders' capital to generate sales, which in turn produce (we hope) profits and cash. The combined figure is return on average equity – earnings per £ of average equity, a crucial measurement of the profitability of the business.

Though sales and profit figures can be manipulated, these numbers all tell us in some way how financially efficient a company is. Reducing them to per-share figures also means that over time, the effects of share issues to "buy" sales, profits, and assets can be factored out of the equation, to leave us with a truer guide.

We can also take a five-year record and look, in respective years at how, for example, *increments* in earnings per share compare with increments in average equity per share. If the ratio of the incremental figures is less than the current level of the ratio, this can indicate that returns are declining.

Here's an example:

Year	1999	2000	2001	2002	2003
Earnings per share	5	7	9	11	12
Incremental eps	–	2	2	2	1
Average equity ps	15	17	19	21	23
Incremental AE	–	2	2	2	2

Over the period, return on equity has increased from 33 percent (5/15) to 52 percent (12/23). On the face of it this looks a respectable enough progression. But look at the latest figures for 2002 and 2003. The increments have varied. Average equity has continued increasing in 2-point increments, but earnings increments have dropped from 2 points to 1 point. This may signal deterioration in future performance and is a clear warning sign. In simple terms, what you want is to invest in a company that is getting steadily better at extracting profit from your (that is, a shareholders') capital.

The jury is out when it comes to a verdict on Hutchison in this respect. The group clearly had a less-than-stellar year in 2001, but a better one in 2002. Earnings per $ of equity in particular is low, just 6 percent or so, but the increment in earnings compares well with the increment in shareholders' equity (HK$0.51 versus HK$1.86), suggesting there is scope for improvement.

Bear in mind, too, that the company's return on equity is relatively low, because it is, in effect, partly a property company. Property investing generates much lower returns than many businesses, but has the benefit of high-quality asset backing.

10 Staff Costs as a Percentage of Sales

THE DEFINITION

This ratio helps investors keep track of a company's employment policies. The ratio shows the total costs of employing all of the staff needed to run the business expressed as a percentage of sales.

THE FORMULA

Staff costs to sales ratio = staff costs × 100/sales

THE COMPONENTS

Staff costs – this is the total cost associated with employing members of staff. It includes not just wages and salaries, but also social security costs (national insurance) and other pension-related costs.

Annual sales – sales, revenue, or turnover are virtually inter-changeable terms. They are in such common use as to need little further explanation. In previous sections we noted that calculations can differ as to whether or not, in performing, you use the sales for the last reported year, or the last 12 months. In this instance, because an up-to-date figure for staff costs is unlikely to be available part way through a year, the sales figure for the latest reported year is the correct one to use.

WHERE'S THE DATA?

Staff costs – the positioning of this information in the accounts varies. It may be stated on the face of the profit and loss account as one of the costs deducted to arrive at operating profit. Or it may occur in a table in the body of the accounts, or (most commonly in the United Kingdom) in a note to the accounts, along with information about numbers of employees.

Annual sales – as noted in previous "magic numbers," this is usually the topmost figure or subtotal in the consolidated profit and loss account or income statement.

CALCULATING IT – THE THEORY

Figure 10.1 shows how the different numbers to be extracted from the accounts combine to produce this particular "magic number."

Figure 10.1   Calculating the "Magic Number" for staff costs as a percentage of sales

Flange Investments Inc. has …

	2003 $m	2002 $m
Wages and salaries of …	20	18
Social security costs of …	1	1
Other pension costs of …	0.5	0.4
Total	**21.5**	**19.4**
Sales of …	130	120
Staff costs as a percentage of sales are …	**16.54%**	**16.17%**
(working)	(21.5 × 100/130)	(19.4 × 100/120)

CALCULATING IT FOR

BAESYSTEMS

Figure 10.2 shows how the highlighted numbers from the 2002 accounts of BAESystems produce the staff-costs-to-sales ratio. BAESystems is the leading British aerospace and defense contractor. There is more information about the company at its web site at *www.baesystems.com*.

Figure 10.2   Calculating it for BaeSystems

The figures ...

Note 5

Aggregate payroll costs of group employees (excluding joint venture employees) were:

	2002 £m	2001 £m	2000 £m
Wages and salaries	2,469	2,451	2,467
Social security costs	203	206	208
Other pension costs	123	158	218
Total	**2,795**	**2,815**	**2,893**

Consolidated profit and loss account

Year to December 31	2002 £m	2001 £m	2000 £m
Sales	12,145	13,138	12,185
less adjustment for share of joint venture sales	−4,069	−4,097	−2,539
Turnover	**8,076**	**9,041**	**9,646**

The calculations ...

Staff costs as a percentage of sales are ...	34.61%	31.14%	29.99%
(working)	(2,795 × 100/8,076)	(2,815 × 100/9,041)	(2,893 × 100/9,646)

With BAESystems we have one of the classic problems that crop up in investing: that of comparing like with like. In this case the complicating factor is that BAESystems has a number of joint ventures. We need to ensure that we compare staff costs and turnover, which in each case relate to activities excluding joint ventures, which are not consolidated in full into the accounts.

Fortunately in this case, this information is readily available.

WHAT IT MEANS

Employees are one of the key costs of any business. Companies need to ensure that they have enough staff to keep customers happy and perform all of the business's essential tasks. But at the same time, they must make sure that payroll and other employment costs do not get out of line with sales and the other expenses of the business. This ratio allows investors to keep track of how efficiently a company is using its staff year by year.

It helps in couple of ways. One way of using it is to monitor how the ratio moves over time. It's worth being suspicious if staff costs as a percentage of sales increase sharply. Equally, comparing this ratio with the one of a close competitor in the same industry can help investors gauge whether or not the company is using its staff efficiently.

There are a couple of drawbacks to this. Because of differences in wage levels from country to country, making valid comparisons of staff costs to sales for companies in different countries is difficult. For example, if we were to take two companies, one in the United Kingdom and one in Brazil, each supplying the airline industry in Europe, it is highly likely that their cost structures would be radically different. The Brazilian company would have cheaper local labor costs, but still earn its turnover in € or £.

Second, under present accounting rules, staff costs as disclosed in a company's accounts do not include the value of employee share options. This issue is being hotly debated at present, and some US companies have moved to treat the value of share options granted in a particular year as a business expense. We'll look at this in more detail in the next "magic number," which deals with management remuneration.

The overwhelming majority of the value of share options grants goes to senior management in a company. Nonetheless, senior management pay is still included in total staff costs. Changes of accounting policy in this area may distort both historical and inter-company comparisons of staff costs to sales.

Finally, there are companies for which the ratio of staff costs to sales assumes particular importance. Chief among these are retailers, where margins can be tight and staff productivity is crucial. Sales and profit per employee are also important in most businesses, and we'll look at these ratios in later "magic numbers."

Directors' Remuneration as a Percentage of Net Income

THE DEFINITION

Directors' pay provokes heated debate. This "magic number" is one way of getting it in perspective. Simply express the aggregate remuneration of directors and officers of the company as a percentage of net income. Why net income? Because this is the figure that should be the "bottom line" of directors' efforts on behalf of company shareholders.

THE FORMULA

Ratio = total directors' and officers' remuneration $\times$ 100/net income

THE COMPONENTS

Net income – this is profit attributable to shareholders after deducting tax and minority interests. Minority interests are the profits that are "owned" by other shareholders in subsidiaries that are less than 100 percent owned.

Directors' and officers' remuneration – this is the total remuneration paid to directors and the senior executive officers in the company (if they are not also directors in their own right). This should include, where applicable, not just salary, but also remuneration from long-term incentive plans and bonuses, and arguably also some value relating to executive share options. Take the total of all the available disclosed items.

WHERE'S THE DATA?

Net income – this is in the profit and loss account (income statement), normally at the bottom of the page. Profit earned for ordinary shareholders (stockholders) should be used. This is the profit figure before any ordinary dividend payments are deducted.

Directors' and officers' remuneration – where this is found varies from company to company.

In the case of UK companies, information on directors' remuneration is usually in the body of the report and accounts, in the notes to the accounts close to the note relating to other staff costs, or else in a separate "report of the compensation committee" section.

In US companies, at the very least the information should be in statutory filings to the SEC's EDGAR system, but it often isn't apparent, or easily identifiable in the annual report.

Once again, Yahoo! Finance (*http://finance.yahoo.com*) has detailed information (sourced from Multex) on directors' and officers' compensation, including the value of exercised, exercisable, and unexercisable share options, and money paid out by long-term incentive plans.

Calculating it — the Theory

Figure 11.1 shows the different numbers to be pulled from the accounts or other data sources, and how to use them to calculate the ratio.

Figure 11.1   Calculating the "Magic Number" for management remuneration as a percentage of net income

Universal Widgets has the following board remuneration ...

	Salary (£000s)	Bonus	Total
Andrew Abel	600	300	900
Bertram Cain	450	200	650
Adam Adams	425	175	600
Eve Adams	200	150	350
Aggregate for all directors			2,500
... and the net income is ...			30,000

That's to say directors' remuneration totals £2.5m and net income is £30m.

Management remuneration as a % of net income is ...	**8.33%**
(working)	(2.5 × 100/30)

CALCULATING IT FOR
GE

Figure 11.2 shows how the highlighted numbers from the accounts of GE combine to produce the figures for directors' remuneration as a percentage of net income. GE is a US-based diversified industrial and financial services company. The company's web site (*www.ge.com*) has more information on the group's operations.

Figure 11.2   Calculating it for GE

The figures (sourced from Yahoo! Finance and Multex) …

Overall officers and directors' compensation (2002) ($000s)

	Total comp.	LTIP	Other	Total
Jeff Immelt	6,949	6,693	796	14,438
Dennis Dammerman	6,776	5,925	501	13,202
Gary Rogers	3,581	4,424	270	8,275
Robert Wright	6,640	10,672	524	17,836
Benjamin Heineman	4,032	3,095	320	7,447
Totals	**27,978**	**30,809**	**2,411**	**61,198**

Net income (2002) $14,118m

The calculation …

Management remuneration as a % of net income is …   0.43%
(working)   (61.2 × 100/14,118)

Care needs to be taken with these numbers because they are so big. Both figures are converted to the standard millions, rather than thousands before the calculation is done. The figure should be eyeballed and double-checked for accuracy.

Looked at another way, the pay of these five individuals collectively amounts to almost one-two-hundredth of the net profits of the company they run.

Aggregate remuneration of these five directors more than doubled in 2002 versus a 3.2% increase in net income.

WHAT IT MEANS

There are problems of definition and elements of considerable controversy surrounding this calculation. For example, the degree to which companies disclose management remuneration differs from country to country.

Board structures also differ. In some countries, like the United States and Germany, directors and officers respectively may be two separate groups of people, and only have a limited number of members in common. In the United Kingdom, all officers are usually directors, although boards also include non-executive directors (who usually get paid much less).

There is a rule of thumb to cut through this confusion. The point of the ratio is to track the remuneration of the people in the company who call the shots when it comes to running the business. Net income measures the bottom line results of their efforts.

Controversy also surrounds the degree to which the value of directors' and officers' share options should be taken into account in the calculation. There are moves afoot (at the time of writing) to treat all annual option grants as remuneration. It is hard to argue otherwise, although some try. Others suggest that the costs should be included only when the options are exercised. When working out directors' remuneration, clearly the *total* value of directors' option holdings is not relevant, since these may include options granted over a period of several years. Equally, they should not be ignored altogether.

The other issue is that this ratio only makes sense when used to compare the remuneration practices of companies of broadly comparable size. It is inevitable that the smaller a company, the greater will be the management remuneration as a percentage of net income. What matters is that companies of similar size and in similar industries are not paying their directors a level of remuneration dramatically out of line with their peers. In addition, if the ratio shoots up from one year to the next – that's to say management pay grows appreciably more than net income – shareholders should justifiably want to know the reason why.

Though lavishly rewarded, management may be providing value for money if it delivers the goods in terms of a rising value attributable to the company. However, simply measuring this by the movement in the share price is facile. Factors that should be taken into account are performance in share price and cash flow terms relative to industry peers, and improvements in returns on shareholders' equity.

12 Sales and Profit Per Employee

THE DEFINITION

Sales and *profit per employee* are ratios that take the normal measures of turnover and profit, and divide them by the average number of employees in the company. The results are measures of employee productivity. They are a particularly good way of measuring the efficiency of "people" businesses.

THE FORMULAS

Sales per employee = net sales/average number of employees in the year

Profit per employee = operating profit/average number of employees in the year

THE COMPONENTS

Annual sales – sales, revenue, or turnover are interchangeable terms and need little further explanation. Where the calculations differ is in whether or not, in performing this calculation, you can take the sales for the last reported year, or the last 12 months.

In practice this calculation needs to be done strictly from the annual accounts of the company in question. This is because although sales figures may be available on a half-yearly or quarter-by-quarter basis, it would be unusual to have the comparable figures for the average numbers of employees.

Operating profit – sometimes called operating income, this is found by taking gross profit and deducting various other items, such as depreciation and amortization, staff costs, and marketing expenditure. Not deducted, at least until the next stage down the income statement, is the income (or losses) attributable to related companies or associates (companies that are less than 50 percent owned), or net interest paid or received.

Operating profit may also include an item, say the profit on the sales for fixed asset investments, which does not relate directly to the mainstream operations of the company. Items like this should be excluded.

It is perhaps also a moot point whether amortization of goodwill should be deducted, since this is a somewhat arbitrary figure devised by accounting standard setters. Depreciation, which reflects wear and tear of fixed tangible assets, is somewhat more clear-cut and the deduction should be included when arriving at operating profit.

Average number of employees – this figure is self-explanatory and is generally fully disclosed by most companies in their accounts. The information is generally not given in quarterly or half-yearly results. Some companies – for example, retailers – that employ a significant number of part-time workers will express the figure in terms of "full-time equivalent" employees, usually basing the calculation on the number of hours worked.

WHERE'S THE DATA?

Annual sales – normally this is the topmost figure or subtotal in the consolidated profit and loss account or income statement. Any sales deriving from large one-off business disposals may distort the figure and should, if appropriate, be excluded. People businesses also sometimes distinguish between gross turnover, which can include spending on behalf of clients, and their own revenue, which purely reflects their fee income. A stockbroker's turnover would, for example, include the value of all the shares bought on behalf of its clients, but true revenue is the commission it earns on those transactions, a much smaller figure.

Operating profit – this is in the income statement and is occasionally called trading profit, although there are some subtle accounting distinctions between the two.

Average number of employees – This is usually in the notes to the accounts, although sometimes in a table in the body of the accounts. Details of payroll costs and staff numbers are often in the same note.

CALCULATING IT – THE THEORY

Table 12.1 shows a fictional example of how the numbers can be used to calculate the ratios in question.

Figure 12.1   Calculating the "Magic Number" for sales and profit per employee

Widget Advertising SA has the following profit and loss account and employee numbers:

Year to December 31 (€m)	2002	2001
Billings	5,000	4,000
Cost of sales	4,000	3,200
Revenue	**1,000**	**800**
Operating costs (excl. goodwill amortization)	750	700
Operating profit	**250**	**100**
Average number of employees	**23,000**	**21,500**
Sales per employee is …	**€43,478**	**€37,209**
(working – thousands omitted)	(1,000,000/23)	(800,000/21.5)
Profit per employee is …	**€10,870**	**€4,651**
(working – thousands omitted)	(250,000/23)	(100,000/21.5)

CALCULATING IT FOR
WPP

Figure 12.2 shows how the highlighted numbers from this extract from the accounts of WPP combine to produce the "magic numbers." WPP is an international advertising agency and marketing services business with operating companies that include J Walter Thompson, Ogilvy & Mather, Hill & Knowlton, and many others. More information on the company can be had from its web site at *www.wpp.com.*

Figure 12.2   Calculating it for WPP

The figures ...

Consolidated profit and loss account for the year ended December, 31 2001

	2001 £m	2000 £m
Turnover (gross billings)	20,887	13,949
Cost of sales	16,865	10,968
Revenue	**4,022**	**2,981**
Direct costs	232	245
Gross profit	3,790	2,736
Operating costs (excl. goodwill amortization)	3,269	2,342
Goodwill amortization and impairment	15	15
Operating profit	506	379

Note 3 **Our people**

Our staff numbers averaged **50,487** against **36,157** in 2000, up 39.6% including acquisitions.

The calculations ...

Operating profit before goodwill amortization is ...	**521**	**394**
(working)	(506 + 15)	(379 + 15)
Sales per employee is ...	**£79,664**	**£82,446**
(working)	(4,022,000/50.487)	(2,981,000/36.157)
Profit per employee is	**£10,319**	**£10,897**
(working)	(521,000/50.487)	(394,000/36.157)

The thousands were omitted in all calculations to aid in computation.

Both in the fictional example and for WPP it is probably quite easy to see that the hardest part of this calculation is making sure that the result is expressed accurately. Bear in mind that turnover and profit figures will frequently be in millions or billions, while employee numbers will generally be in thousands. If in doubt, it is worth performing the calculations in full on a calculator, at least initially.

In other words, in the case of Widget Advertising we enter 1,000,000,000 in the calculator and divide by 23,000. When reading off the result, pay particular attention to the position of commas and decimal points in the display.

Once we have established the approximate order of magnitude of the likely result, simply dividing the two numbers is sufficient, since the correct figure will be much more obvious in a subsequent calculation.

There remain some problems that are often encountered when calculating the ratio. One is that it is essential that only true turnover and profit attributable to the business itself is included. In instances where companies have 50 percent owned joint ventures, different accounting methods may be used to determine turnover.

In this instance it is important to ensure that the ratios are not distorted. If employee numbers exclude joint venture employees, then sales and profit figures should exclude the amounts derived from this source as well.

WHAT IT MEANS

In the end, companies stand or fall by the quality of their employees and by the sales and profit these individuals generate for shareholders. These ratios are particularly important for businesses that rely heavily on people to supply their stock in trade.

The ratio is therefore a good way of measuring any financial organization, retailer, consultant, software company, or advertising agency. The ratios are less important than some other key financial ratios like return on capital – but they are important. It is particularly useful to look at the ratios over a period of years to see whether there have been any noticeable trends.

The ratios also show up differences between competitors in key "people" businesses. They show up quite clearly, too, how acquisitions can affect the numbers for sales and profit per employee. In the example of WPP, the acquisition during 2001 of Young & Rubicam resulted not only in a sharp increase in the overall number of employees, but also a decline in both turnover and profit per employee.

The changes were marginal and with WPP's expert financial management, the clear hope is that the new parent will be able to raise overall employee productivity back to previous levels after a year or two. The ratio identifies the problem area clearly.

13

"Pro-forma" Earnings

THE DEFINITION

"Pro-forma" earnings are those that are calculated "as if" certain adjustments, required by normal accounting standards, had not been made. Often this means earnings that exclude charges that would otherwise have depressed earnings and includes items that make the figures look better.

THE FORMULA

"Pro-forma" earnings = statutory earnings − exceptional debits + exceptional credits

In other words, exceptional and non-trading debits charged to statutory earnings are added back, and exceptional and non-trading credits excluded from statutory earnings are included in "pro-forma" ones. In both cases, the adjustment made should also allow for the tax effect of these items, if any.

THE COMPONENTS

Statutory earnings – this is a catch-all term. Statutory earnings are frequently referred to by the designation of the relevant accounting principles used in their compilation. The term used in the United States and in many other areas is GAAP. This stands for "generally accepted accounting principles." In the United Kingdom the term FRS3 is used. This refers to Financial Reporting Standard 3, the accounting standard that governs the preparation of the income statement.

Exceptional (and non-trading) debits – these are charges that would reduce reported profits prepared under statutory accounting conventions. They include a variety of items, as varied as the imaginings the company's accountants can dream up.

Typical charges might be, for example, goodwill amortization, losses on disposal of property assets, restructuring and redundancy costs, amounts written off investments, losses on foreign exchange, shortfalls on pension fund liabilities, losses generated by companies that have since been sold, and a range of other items.

Exceptional (and non-trading) credits – these are credits that increase reported profits, but which do not arise from the normal day-to-day trading of the company. They might for, example, include a gain on sale of investments, a gain on sale of a property, profits generated by companies that have since been sold, gains on foreign exchange, and a range of other items.

WHERE'S THE DATA?

Statutory earnings – this figure is contained on the face of the income statement (profit and loss account). You can identify it by looking for a phrase that states that the statement has been prepared under generally accepted accounting principles or gives the name of the relevant accounting standard.

This information may be contained in a note to the accounts, or in the summary of accounting policies that will form part of the accounts. If the words "adjusted," restated, or "pro-forma" are used, what follows are almost certainly *not* the figures prepared according to statutory accounting conventions. By process of elimination it is usually possible to get to the most conservatively compiled figure.

Wherever possible, take the data from a company's annual report and accounts, which is a statutory document. Do not use a news release, because it is not a statutory document. If using a news release is unavoidable, bear in mind that the statutory figures may be confined to a note at the back of the release. Much more prominence may be given to adjusted, restated, or "pro-forma" numbers. This has been particularly true in the past of some US companies.

Exceptional debits and credits – items like this are typically either on the face of the income statement or in the notes to the accounts. In the United Kingdom, recent changes to accounting standards (FRS14 – introduced December 1998) largely abolished the earlier distinction between exceptional and extraordinary items (where the latter could legitimately be excluded from earnings calculations). All exceptional items are now disclosed on the face of the profit and loss account. An additional distinction is also drawn between those that arise from acquisitions and disposals of businesses.

Accounting conventions in the United States and elsewhere may not require such detailed disclosure on the face of the income statement, but the relevant information is usually in the notes to the accounts. For US companies the form 10K, the statutory filing that US companies have to make to the SEC, is the most complete disclosure. Filings such as this are often at company web sites and at the SEC's EDGAR web site.

CALCULATING IT – THE THEORY

Table 13.1 shows a fictional example of how the highlighted numbers can be used to calculate "pro-forma" earnings.

Figure 13.1   Calculating the "Magic Number" for "pro-forma" earnings

Widget Software has the following profit and loss account numbers.

Year to December 31 (£m)	2002	2001
Net sales	500	400
Cost of sales	300	250
Gross profit	200	150
Operating expenses:		
Sales and marketing	100	80
General and administrative	50	40
Restructuring costs	**10**	**20**
Issue of share options to staff	**25**	**10**
Amortization of goodwill	**10**	**10**
Profit on sale of properties	−20	−20
Operating profit	25	10
Net interest	15	8
Pre-tax profit	10	2
Tax	3	1
Net profit attributable	**7**	**1**
Weighted average shares in issue (m)	**150**	**150**
Reported earnings per share	4.7p	0.67p

"Pro-forma" earnings per share calculated as follows:

1. Amount to add back to get to "pro-forma"
   operating profit   45   40
   (working) $(10 + 25 + 10)$ $(20 + 10 + 10)$

   Only costs are excluded. Property profits, though clearly exceptional, are kept in.

2. Adjust for tax by applying tax rate to figure
   added back   31.5   20
   (working) $(45 \times (1 - 0.3))$ $(40 \times (1 - 0.5))$

3. Add back adjusted amount to net profit attributable   38.5   21
   (working) $(31.5 + 7.0)$ $(20 + 1)$

4. Calculate "pro-forma" eps in the usual way   25.7p   14p
   (working) $(38.5/150)$ $(21/150)$

We have calculated this by assuming that all the exceptional items are in fact allowable as tax deductions. In reality this may not always be the case. Where loss-making (and therefore non-taxpaying) companies use "pro-forma" calculation, tax adjustments need not be made.

Interpretations vary. Some companies would exclude the property profits item from "pro-forma" earnings. Mostly, however, when working out "pro-forma" earnings, they remove all of the one-time and inconvenient charges they can, and include all of the extra income that can possibly be included. Not for nothing are "pro-forma" earnings sometimes known as "earnings before all the bad stuff."

CALCULATING IT FOR

AMAZON

Figure 13.2 shows an extract from the Q3 2002 accounts of Amazon to illustrate how this company arrives at "pro-forma" earnings. Amazon is of course the pre-eminent online retailer. More information on the company is available at *www.amazon.com* (look in the "about us" section of the site.)

Let's stress from the outset that Amazon plays the issue of "pro-forma" reporting of earnings with a considerable degree of integrity and consistency, giving due weight in its press releases, both to the profits under GAAP and to how the numbers look under "pro-forma" reporting.

We have chosen Amazon for this example because its accounts show particularly clearly how "pro-forma" earnings are arrived at in an actual case and how considerably they may differ from the reported figures.

It is also worth recalling that the financial press and news channels at the time of these results reported faithfully that Amazon had made a profit on this occasion. This particular headline was the one that stuck in the mind. The financial press largely failed to note that the profit was only struck, as the example shows, after a large number of items were excluded from the calculation.

Figure 13.2 Calculating it for Amazon.com

The figures and calculation ...

Amazon.com Inc. – "Pro-forma" statement of operations ($000)

Three months ended September 30

	2002 Reported	2002 Adj.	2002 Pro-forma	2001 Reported	2001 Adj.	2001 Pro-forma
Net sales	851,299		851,299	639,281		639,281
Cost of sales	635,132		635,132	477,089		477,089
Gross profit	216,167		216,167	162,192		162,192
Operating expenses						
Fulfillment	90,342		90,342	81,400		81,400
Marketing	26,728		26,728	32,537		32,537
Technology and content	52,907		52,907	53,846		53,846
General and administrative	18,698		18,698	21,481		21,481
Stock-based compensation	–832	832	0	–2,567	2,567	0
Amortization of goodwill	1,212	–1,212	0	41,835	–41,835	0
Restructuring related and other	36,757	–36,757	0	3,994	–3,994	0
Income from operations	–9,645	37,137	27,492	–70,334	43,262	–27,072
Interest income	5,600		5,600	6,316		6,316
Interest expense	–35922		–35,922	–35,046		–35,046
Other income/(expense)	3,183		3,183	–2,203		–2,203
Other gains/(losses)	2,261	–2,261	0	–63,625	63,625	0
Income before related companies	–34,523	34,876	353	–164,892	106,887	–58,005
Share in related companies' losses	–557	557	0	–4,982	4,982	0
Net income	**–35,080**	**35,433**	**353**	**–169,874**	**111,869**	**–58,005**
Income/(loss) per share	–0.09	0.09	0.00	–0.46	0.30	–0.16

The reported earnings-per-share figure for the third-quarter against the same period of the previous year was a loss of 9 cents versus a loss of 46 cents. In "pro-forma" terms it was breakeven compared to a loss of 16 cents a share.

These figures do not, however, adequately convey the scale of the adjustment. In Q3 2002, for example, the total adjustments to get from reported to "pro-forma" were some $35 million and a whopping $112 million in the same period of the previous year. Remember that these numbers are for a single quarter only. The size of the adjustment in Q3 2001, for example, represented 17.5 percent of sales in that quarter. In Q2 2002 the adjustment was greater than the entire net loss made by the group in the period.

While Amazon did also in fairness adjust for some exceptional credits in the periods in question, one really has to ask whether profit figures after adjustments of this magnitude can really claim to be any improvement on figures produced under conventional accounting guidelines. Nor can they be said to offer analysts and investors any more meaningful guide to performance than the officially sanctioned ones.

WHAT IT MEANS

You may think we have adopted a somewhat cynical tone here. However, it was a feature of the bull market of the 1990s that many companies, particularly in the United States, used the idea of "pro-forma" earnings to present investors with a more favorable profit picture than would have been the case had they simply reported the profit figures required under international or US accounting standards.

"Pro-forma" earnings presented in this way carry no legal weight. Company filings, and indeed their official profit announcements, in the United States and elsewhere must contain (even if only in an appendix to the news release) an income statement that presents results on the basis of GAAP (generally accepted accounting principles).

Companies justify the use of "pro-forma" earnings because they claim that the practice gives investors a better view of the ongoing profit potential of the business. But more often the impression is that the use of this practice is at best self-serving and at worst positively misleading. The use of "pro-forma" earnings, in which analysts and financial newspapers and news channels willingly and uncritically participated, without doubt led many investors to an unduly rosy view of company profitability and therefore led them to place an excessive value on their shares.

Having said that, there are legitimate uses of the "pro-forma" technique. This is most notably the case in major takeovers. In this case, the technique can be applied to both the income statement and also the balance sheet.

When the results of a company are published at the end of a year during which a major takeover has taken place, companies will sometimes restate their results so as to provide an *additional* income statement that gives the turnover and profit figures for the combined company, as if the takeover had been made at the beginning of the financial year and the results of the acquired company had been included for a full 12 months.

The benefit of this exercise comes in subsequent years when the "pro-forma" figure can provide a more meaningful comparison with the sales and profit figures in the years that follow.

From a balance sheet standpoint, "pro-forma" statements of combined net assets are also often used in the small print of offer documents, to show what the balance sheet effects of a takeover would be on the bidding company's balance sheet, once the target company's assets and liabilities have been included, and all the share issues and borrowings needed to finance the takeover have been made.

This is often an important consideration for investors who will want to decide whether or not to vote in favor of the takeover. They may wish to continue to participate in the shares of the merged company if they like what they see. Or they may sell their shares if they believe that the move may place an undue strain on the financial resources of the company. In these circumstances "pro-forma" financial statements serve a useful purpose.

In the United Kingdom there is the additional concept of "normalized" earnings. This takes statutory earnings (known in the United Kingdom as FRS3 earnings – after the Financial Reporting Standard that prescribes how they should be drawn up) and adjusts for non-trading profits and losses, and for exceptional credit and debits.

In the calculation, non-trading losses and exceptional charges are added back to reported statutory earnings, and non-trading profits and exceptional profits are deducted in order to eliminate their effect. Weighted average shares in issue are then used in the normal way to arrive at earnings per share.

There is always a trade-off between showing the unvarnished figures prepared in strict accordance with accounting standards, and those that remove what may be transient items which will distort comparisons with either prior or subsequent years. Investors should always be intensely skeptical when management gives undue prominence to "pro-forma" or adjusted earnings in their publicity material and news releases. The best companies simply provide all of the information in a clear way and allow investors to make up their own minds which figure is the best to use.

14 Margins

THE DEFINITION

For margins, read "profit margins." Margins are measures of profitability found by dividing a profit figure by sales revenue. The profit and loss account (or income statement) contains several different measures of profit. So in turn there are several ways of calculating margins. These are:

Gross margin – this is the percentage that gross profit represents of sales revenue.

Operating margin – this is the percentage that operating profit represents of sales revenue.

Pre-tax margin – this is the percentage that profit before tax represents of sales revenue.

Some US analysts also use net margin (net profit after tax and minorities expressed as a percentage of sales). We have, however, not included the calculation in the example, for reasons explained below.

THE FORMULAS

Gross margin = (gross profit × 100)/sales revenue

Operating margin = (operating profit × 100)/sales revenue

Pre-tax margin = (pre-tax profit × 100)/sales revenue

Net margin is pre-tax profit multiplied by 100 and divided by sales.

THE COMPONENTS

Sales – sales, revenue, or turnover are interchangeable terms, and are in such common use as to need little further explanation. Calculations can differ over whether or not you take the sales for the last reported year, or for the last 12 months. The latter may include sales for half-years or quarters that have elapsed since the previous financial year-end.

Margins can be calculated for part of a year – provided that the profit figure for a particular period is compared with the sales figure for the same period.

Gross profit – imagine the income statement as a column that starts with sales, from which items are deducted successively to arrive at different levels of profit, the bottom-most item being retained profit. Gross profit is always the topmost profit figure quoted in the income statement (although some accounts omit it altogether, proceeding directly to operating profit – see below). Gross profit is normally defined as sales revenue minus the cost of sales. The term "cost of sales" means the cost of any bought-in raw materials or components.

Operating profit – sometimes called operating income, this is the next level down in the profit "column." Companies calculate it by taking gross profit and deducting various other items. These include depreciation and amortization, staff costs, and sales and marketing expenditure. Not deducted, at least until the next stage, is income (or losses) attributable to related companies (these are companies that are less than 50 percent owned), or net interest paid or received.

Pre-tax profit – this is operating income after deducting (or crediting as appropriate) any remaining items down to, but not including, tax.

Net profit is the bottom-most profit figure in the income statement column, taken immediately before dividends are deducted to arrive at retained earnings. Because net profit varies with the corporate tax regime, which is to some degree outside the control of the company, it can differ from country to country. For this reason its usefulness for international comparisons is limited.

WHERE'S THE DATA?

Sales – this is normally the topmost figure or subtotal in the consolidated profit and loss account or income statement.

Gross profit – if separately calculated this is also in the income statement a couple of lines below the sales (turnover, or revenue) figure.

Operating profit – operating profit is a little further down the income statement and is occasionally called trading profit, although there are some subtle accounting distinctions between the two. Trading profit tends to correspond to profit before interest (sometimes called EBIT – earnings before interest and tax) and may include items, say the profit on the sales of fixed asset investments, which do not relate directly to the mainstream operations of the company.

Pre-tax profit – this is in the income statement immediately *above* the tax line. It is a matter of debate whether or not you include non-trading or extraordinary items from the margin calculation. If you exclude items like this from profit, then you must also exclude the revenue relating to them from the sales figure you use to calculate margins.

Net profit is toward the bottom of the income statement immediately *above* the dividend line.

CALCULATING IT – THE THEORY

Figure 14.1 shows the different numbers to be pulled from the accounts and how to use them to calculate the ratio. For reasons explained above, we have not included net margin in the calculation.

Figure 14.1   Calculating the "Magic Number" for margins

Flangewerke Deutscheland AG has an income statement that looks like this ...

Year to December 31 (€m)	2002
Turnover	200
less Cost of sales	60
Gross profit	140
less Operating expenses	70
Operating profit	70
less Interest paid	20
Pre-tax profit	50
less Taxation	20
Profit after tax	30
less Minority interests	2
Profit attributable to shareholders	28
less Dividends	8
Retained profits	20
Gross margin is ...	**70%**
(working)	$(140 \times 100)/200$
Operating margin is ...	**35%**
(working)	$(70 \times 100)/200$
Pre-tax margin is ...	**25%**
(working)	$(50 \times 100)/200$

CALCULATING IT FOR
CLP HOLDINGS

Figure 14.2 shows how the highlighted numbers from this extract from the accounts of CLP combine to produce the "magic numbers." CLP Holdings is the holding company for China Light & Power. The company is a leading investor and operator in the Asia-Pacific electric power sector. More information on the company can be found on its web site at *www.clpgroup.com*.

Figure 14.2   Calculating margins from CLP Holding's 2002 accounts

The figures ...

Financial results

	2002 HK$m	2001 HK$m
Turnover	26,134	24,999
Expenses		
Purchases of electricity – Capco	10,191	9,815
Purchases of electricity – Daya Bay	4,976	5,013
Pumped storage fee	419	424
Staff expenses	945	929
Other operating costs	1,331	1,246
Depreciation	1,749	1,624
Property disposal gain	313	0
Operating profit	6,836	5,948
Finance costs	−189	−187
Finance income	33	29
Hok Un redevelopment profit	282	1,752
Share of joint venture profits	2,976	2,339
Share of associated company profits	86	71
Profit before taxation	10,024	9,952

The calculations ...

Gross margin is ...	**40.4%**	**39.0%**

(working for 2001) (24,999 − 9,815 − 5,013 − 424) × 100/24,999
(working for 2002) (26,134 − 10,191 − 4,976 − 419) × 100/26,134

Gross profit is turnover less external expenses, in this case bought-in power and pumping costs. Once calculated, this figure is expressed as a percentage of sales.

Operating margin is ...	26.2%	23.8%
(working)	$(6,836 \times 100)/26,134$	$(5,948 \times 100)/24,999$
Pre-tax margin is ...	38.4%	39.8%
(working)	$(10,024 \times 100)/26,134$	$(9,952 \times 100)/24,999$

Pre-tax margin is higher than operating margin because of the inclusion of profit shares from joint venture and related companies. Turnover from these ventures may not have been included.

CLP's accounts are not particularly straightforward when it comes to calculating margins.

In the first place, cost of sales is not shown as a separate item and therefore gross profit has to be calculated from the information given in the accounts. It can, however, be estimated by deducting those operating expenses that are patently external to the group. In this case, these are the costs of bought-in power and pumping.

At the operating profit level, a case could be made for excluding the property disposal gain. If so, this would give adjusted operating profits of HK$6,836 million and operating margins of 24.95 percent in 2002, rather than the 26.2 percent calculated in the example.

A more obvious adjustment could be made at the pre-tax margin stage, by stripping out the share of profits from joint ventures and those from associated companies. The reason for doing this would not be that they are not legitimate sources of profit, but that the share of turnover related to some of them may not have been included in the company turnover figure.

Without minute scrutiny of the full report and accounts (not available at the time of writing), or a conversation with the finance director or an investor relations executive, it would be hard to determine precisely how to make the adjustment. It means that pre-tax margins and trends in them need to be treated with caution in this case.

WHAT IT MEANS

Margins are important indicators of the health of a business. They are at their most revealing when comparisons are made either between companies, or over an extended period of time (say, five financial years) at the same company. This allows the all-important trend in margins to be established.

What should you look for? In short, margins that are either steady or rising gently. Falling margins can be a sign of problems, especially if the company or the industry involved is not cyclical. This is because margin numbers show the extent to which the company is able to pass on bought-in costs in its prices to customers (gross margin), and the extent to which it has its own internal costs under control (operating margin).

Gross margins are also an indicator of value added – the higher the gross margin, the more value the company itself is adding to raw materials and bought-in inputs.

They are, however, higher in some industries than others.

Retailers, for example, are often judged on their margin performance. Food retailing companies, which depend on high throughput of goods and keen prices, operate on low gross margins. However, they can take money from customers at the checkout instantly, yet take advantage of extended credit periods from their suppliers, over whom they exert considerable power.

Software companies, which license their intellectual property and have few bought-in costs, have high gross margins.

What do we mean by "high" and "low"? Gross margins of 70–80 percent or more would be considered high. Those below, say, 30 percent would be considered low.

CLP falls somewhere between the two extremes on gross margins. Its operating margins look respectable.

Part Three

Cash Flow Statement "Magic Numbers"

CASH FLOW STATEMENT "MAGIC NUMBERS"

Cash is king. And what's important about the "magic numbers" based around a company's cash flow statement is that, unlike profits, they cannot be fudged, smoothed, or manipulated.

If in doubt, look to the cash flow statement to find out what really happened. Were a company's profits artificially high because of changes in depreciation policy? Were they inflated because the company was producing for stock? Or did the company have to pay its bills more slowly or grant customers more favorable credit terms?

Some of the "magic numbers" in this section are easy to work out, but crucial for evaluating a company's financial strength. Others are slightly more complex.

- Compare operating cash flow with operating profit and you get a view of how efficiently a company's profits translate into cash. Almost all companies should have operating cash flow in excess of operating profits.

- Price to cash flow is the cash flow statement's counterpart to the PE ratio. It uses free cash flow, rather than earnings, as the bottom half of the fraction. Free cash flow is operating cash flow less interest, tax, and capital spending. This ratio needs careful interpretation, but it is a more reliable (although less commonly used) indicator.

- A similar ratio compares free cash flow to sales. This is the counterpart to the margin figures we looked at earlier, but uses net profits in cash terms as its basis. The value of this figure is that it is less easy for unscrupulous management teams to fudge.

- Cash flow return on invested capital takes after-tax operating cash flow and expresses it as a percentage of total assets less non-interest-bearing current liabilities. This is the cash flow counterpart to the return on capital calculation covered in the next section. Like other cash flow ratios, it derives its value from the reliability of cash flow as an indicator of financial health. When compared with weighted average cost of capital, it can be a key indicator of a company's financial health.

- Finally, discounted cash flow is a widely used valuation technique that projects cash flow into the future and discounts each successive year's value back to the present to establish what the company should be worth today. This is a more complex calculation and it does have its limitations. However, it is one of the essential tools to master when looking at a company.

Not all of these numbers are applicable to every company, although price to cash flow and operating cash flow to operating profit tend to work well for most.

The pivotal role cash and cash flow-related numbers play in assessing whether or not a company is sound explains why some companies are reluctant to display too much detail. In many countries, cash flow statements are an afterthought. It is common for companies not to give cash flow numbers at the halfway stage of the year.

Some argue that cash flow is a more difficult concept to grasp. Anyone who has run a business, however small, will understand its significance. The real reason for the reluctance of some parts of the financial community and the financial press to use cash flow measures is that some analysts, journalists, and broadcasters are by nature lazy. They prefer the easy shorthand of earnings per share and measures based on them, however flawed they may be, to the slightly more complex idea of cash flow.

The result is that these ratios are not used as often as they should be by both professional investors and private investors alike. As we noted in the original *Magic Numbers* book, you can get a real edge in stock selection if you persevere with them.

15 Operating Cash Flow/ Operating Profit

THE DEFINITION

You calculate this ratio by dividing cash flow from operations (from the cash flow statement) by operating profit (from the income statement). In all normal circumstances, cash flow from operations should be more than operating profit. So the ratio should always exceed one.

THE FORMULA

Ratio = operating cash flow/operating profit

THE COMPONENTS

Operating cash flow – sometimes called "net cash from operating activities" or "net cash inflow from operating activities," this figure adjusts operating profit for items that affect the way profit is calculated, but that do not represent movements of cash. These items include depreciation and amortization; provisions; retained profits of related companies; and changes in debtors, creditors, and stocks. Most companies show the derivation of operating cash flow in detail.

Operating profit – sometimes called operating income, this is gross profit less various other items such as depreciation and amortization, staff costs, and sales and marketing expenditure. Income (or losses) attributable to related companies, or net interest paid or received, is not deducted, at least until the next stage down the income statement.

The term "related companies" crops up in both places. The definition of related (or "associated") companies is strict. They are companies that are less than 50 percent, but more than 20 percent owned, and where the main "parent" company exerts some management control, perhaps through a director on the board. Companies can include their share of the profits of companies like this, but except for any dividends that might be paid, receive no flows of cash from them.

WHERE'S THE DATA?

Operating cash flow – this is in the cash flow statement toward the top of the page. Avoid confusing the figure for operating cash flow with operating profit (see below). Cash flow tables often start with operating profit – taken from the income statement – as the topmost figure. They then show how the various adjustments produce operating cash flow. In other cases, this reconciliation of the two figures is in a note.

Operating profit – this is in the income statement and is occasionally called trading profit. There are some subtle accounting distinctions between the two. Trading profit tends to correspond to profit before interest (sometimes called EBIT – earnings before interest and tax). It may include an item, say the profit on the sales of fixed asset investments, which does not relate directly to the mainstream operations of the company. Items like this should, if possible, be excluded from operating profit.

CALCULATING IT – THE THEORY

Figure 15.1 shows the different numbers to be pulled from the accounts and how to use them to calculate the ratio.

Figure 15.1   Calculating the "Magic Number" for operating cash flow/operating profit

Widget Stores plc has the following note to its cash flow statement:	
	£m
Operating profit	420
Exceptional items	−20
	400
Depreciation	300
(Increase)/decrease in stocks	−25
(Increase)/decrease in debtors	35
(Increase)/decrease in creditors	20
Increase in provisions	5
Net cash inflow from operating activities	735
Operating cash flow/operating profit is …	**1.75**
(working)	(735/420)

CALCULATING IT FOR
GlaxoSmithKline

Figure 15.2 shows how the highlighted numbers from this extract from the accounts of GlaxoSmithKline combine to produce the "magic number." GlaxoSmithKline is a leading global pharmaceutical company. More information about the company is at *www.gsk.com.*

Figure 15.2 Calculating it for GlaxoSmithKline

The figures ...

GlaxoSmithKline has the following item in its cash flow statement (p. 78):

Reconciliation of operating profit to operating cash flow

	2002 £m	2001 £m	2000 £m
Operating profit	**5,551**	**4,734**	**4,729**
Depreciation	764	761	735
Impairment and assets written off	288	178	136
Amortization of goodwill	72	50	38
Loss on sale of tangible fixed assets	26	99	41
Profit on sale of equity investments	−46	−118	−225
(Increase)/decrease in stocks	−2	252	−16
Increase in trade and other debtors	−72	−77	−333
Increase in trade and other creditors	459	601	402
Increase in pension and other provisions	256	144	70
Other	−41	−93	−39
Merger transaction costs	0	−24	−97
Net cash inflow from operating activities	**7,255**	**6,507**	**5,441**

The calculations ...

	2002	2001	2000
Operating cash flow/operating profit is ...	**1.31**	**1.37**	**1.15**
(working)	(7,255/5,551)	(6,507/4,734)	(5,441/4,729)

The calculation is straightforward in the case of GSK. The note reproduced in Figure 15.2 provides a good illustration of the items deducted and credited in the process of getting from operating profit to operating cash flow. GSK is a model company in the sense that its disclosed profits are consistently less than operating cash flow. This indicates that no attempts have been made to flatter profits by manipulating book entry items or working capital.

WHAT IT MEANS

The example shows very logically how changes in working capital and the size of the depreciation charge and other book entries produce the difference between operating profit and operating cash flow. GSK's accounting layout is a textbook example.

Not all companies are as clear as this. So above all, remember that like should be compared with like. Operating profit is simply adjusted for the non-cash items (depreciation, amortization, and provisions) that are deducted in the process of arriving at operating profit. Operating cash flow should not therefore be calculated after tax, interest, dividends, and the like, because none of these items is deducted from operating profit.

The beauty of this ratio, which reflects the efficiency with which profits are converted into cash, is that it is simple to calculate. The ratio speaks volumes about the integrity of the company and the honesty of its accounting. Because depreciation and other non-cash charges are added back, operating cash flow should always be higher than operating profit. If it is not, it usually means there has been deterioration in working capital ratios.

Companies that have cash conversion ratios of less than 100 percent are on a slippery slope, because they are generating less cash than their income statement implies. Conversely, the more the ratio exceeds 100 percent, the more profits are being "hidden" (perhaps by a very conservative depreciation policy) and the better the investment is likely to prove.

The ratio works for all types of companies. It is also good to compare the operating cash flow to operating profit ratio over a period of years, to make sure that the figures are consistent and not simply showing an unsustainable one-off improvement. Differences between companies generally reflect the conservatism or otherwise of management in calculating depreciation and other non-cash items, and the efficiency with which working capital is used.

16 Price to Free Cash Flow Ratio

The Definition

Rather like the PE ratio, the *price to free cash flow ratio (PCF)* compares the share price with free cash flow per share (rather than earnings per share). Alternatively, market capitalization can be divided by free cash flow, although this method is marginally less accurate.

The Formulas

PCF = share price/(free cash flow/weighted average shares in issue)

Or, slightly less accurately:

PCF = market capitalization/free cash flow

The latter calculation is easier and quicker to do, but because market capitalization comprises the latest shares in issue (rather than the weighted average) multiplied by the current share price, the resulting ratio may be less accurate.

The Components

Share (stock) price – this is the current market price of the shares, normally the mid-market price at the close of business on the previous trading day.

Free cash flow – all cash flow calculations ignore book-entry transactions and concentrate purely on the flows of cash into and out of a business. Hence, they ignore depreciation, amortization of goodwill, retained profits of minority-owned companies, and capitalized interest. Strictly speaking, free cash flow also deducts those items that a company cannot avoid paying if it wants to stay in business: interest, tax, and sufficient capital spending to maintain its fixed assets. So free cash flow is operating cash flow less interest paid, tax paid, and "maintenance" capital spending.

Weighted average shares in issue – the time-weighted average number of shares in issue during the year. The shares concerned are those that have been issued and are publicly listed.

Allow for any stock splits that may have taken place after the date the accounts were drawn up. The calculation of the weighted average is normally performed on a monthly basis. For example, an increased number of shares in issue that took place eight months into the year would have a weighting of 4/12 in the calculation (because four months of the year remain), while the original number of shares in issue at the start of the year would have a weighting of 8/12.

Market capitalization (for a quick version of calculation) – issued shares multiplied by the share price.

Where's the Data?

Share (stock) price – from any daily newspaper or financial web site.

Free cash flow – most of the components of free cash flow (for example, operating cash flow, interest paid, and tax paid) are in the cash flow statement. Avoid confusing the figure for operating cash flow with that of operating profit. Cash flow tables often start with operating profit as the topmost figure and then show how the various adjustments produce operating cash flow.

Capital spending is in the cash flow statement or the notes relating to it, under the heading "net cash outflow for capital expenditure, purchase of fixed assets, and financial investment" – or some combination of these words. Payments for acquisitions (usually termed "purchase of subsidiaries" and the like) and any suspiciously large one-off items can be ignored. Maintenance capital spending is generally assumed to be around one-half or two-thirds of total capital spending.

Weighted average shares in issue – this is generally in the note to the accounts referring to the earnings-per-share calculation. Earnings per share are often calculated for investors and stated at the foot of the income statement. The note will normally disclose the weighted average number of shares used as the basis for the calculation. The weighted average used for calculating earnings per share can equally be used for working out free cash flow per share.

Market capitalization – normally published in the financial press or at financial web sites like Yahoo! Finance.

CALCULATING IT – THE THEORY

Figure 16.1 shows the different numbers to be pulled from the accounts and how to use them to calculate the ratio.

Figure 16.1   Calculating the "Magic Number" for price to free cash flow per share

Universal Widgets Pte. has the following cash flow and income statement items:

	S$m
Net cash inflow from operations	100
Depreciation	20
Amortization of goodwill	25
Interest paid	−15
Tax paid	−22
Purchases of fixed assets	−17
Sales of fixed assets	2
Free cash flow before capital spend is ...	63
(working)	(100 − 15 − 22)
Maintenance capital spending is ...	−10
(working)	two-thirds (say) of (−17 + 2)
Free cash flow is ...	53
(working)	(63 − 10)
Weighted average shares in issue are ...	10.0m
Current shares in issue are ...	10.5m
Share price is ...	S$50
Free cash flow per share is ...	S$5.30
(working)	(53/10)
Price to FCF per share is ...	**9.4**
(working)	(50/5.30)
Price to FCF (quick calculation) is ...	**9.9**
(working)	((50 × 10.5)/53)

In the quick calculation, market capitalization (based on current shares in issue) is divided by free cash flow in millions of dollars. Because of the difference between weighted shares in issue and the current figure, the result is noticeably different.

CALCULATING IT FOR
MICROSOFT

Figure 16.2 shows how the highlighted numbers from this extract from the accounts of Microsoft combine to produce the "magic number."

Figure 16.2   Calculating it for Microsoft

Microsoft's fiscal 2002 cash flow statement shows the following items:

	$m
Net cash inflow from operations	14,509
Tax paid (already deducted from the above figure)	4,210
Interest paid (already deducted from the above figure)	0
Purchases of fixed assets	770
Sales of fixed assets	0
Free cash flow before capital spend is ...	14,509
Maintenance capital spending is ... (working)	516 (two-thirds (say) of 770)
Free cash flow is ... (working)	13,993 (14,509 − 516)
Weighted average shares in issue are ...	10.8bn
Current shares in issue are ...	10.7bn
Share price is ...	$26.21
Free cash flow per share is ... (working – in billions)	**$1.30** (13.993/10.8)
Price to FCF per share is ... (working)	**20.2** (26.21/1.30)
Price to FCF (quick calculation) is ... (working – in billions)	**20.0** ((26.21 × 10.7)/13.993)

Some US companies reconcile cash flow and profits slightly differently, taking net income as the basis and then adding back non-cash items. UK companies work the other way round, starting from pre-interest profit. They deduct payments like tax and interest, and add back book entries like depreciation and amortization.

You need to pay attention to these distinctions because you do not want to deduct tax and interest again, if these deductions are already reflected in the base figure.

This is actually the case with Microsoft, as Figure 16.2 shows. Microsoft's extensive financial assets mean it has no interest payments to deduct. As the cash flow reconciliation starts using net (that is, after-tax) income as the basis, tax does not have to be deducted again.

Finally, since the company has been buying back shares, the current shares in issue are slightly lower than the number of the weighted average. Both figures have been adjusted to allow for a two-for-one stock split that took place in mid-February 2003.

All of these elements in the calculation demonstrate the need to think clearly and logically when performing calculations like this. Do not simply follow the formula mechanically.

What it Means

Like the PE ratio, PCF is a key ratio for analysts and investors alike. One way of looking at it is that it represents the number of years of free cash flow at the current rate before the price of the shares is recouped. This idea is only notional, because the cash flow will not be returned in full to shareholders.

A more meaningful way of looking at it is now being used by some analysts. This is the concept of the "free cash flow yield." This is simply the reciprocal of the price to free cash flow ratio. An investment with a price to free-cash-flow ratio of 12.5 times, for example, would have a free-cash-flow yield of 8 percent. The advantage of the free cash flow yield is that it can be compared with the cash return on other investments.

Like the PER (or earnings yield), the important aspect of the PCF is that it enables companies to be compared irrespective of their size, the concept reducing each company to a common currency. This is important because it will, for example, enable the stock market rating of an individual company to be compared with its competitors, and with the market.

Prospective (that is, forecast) cash flows are often used to calculate the PCF. Although less widely studied than earnings or sales revenues, the market sets some store by these predictions. As we noted earlier, one reason why some stock market analysts are paid the huge amounts they are is because of a supposed skill in forecasting earnings and cash flow.

However good they may be, various factors conspire to make cash flow per share less predictable than earnings per share. The trend in cash flow may be more erratic than earnings for reasons that may lie outside the control of the company.

The virtue of free cash flow is, however, that it is a more objective measure of the worth of a company, less liable to be "fudged" or "smoothed." Changes in accounting policies, and not least the ingenuity of analysts in manipulating earnings calculations to suit the case they wish to make, do mean that cash flow per share is increasingly, and rightly, seen as a more reliable means of judging whether or not a company is undervalued or overvalued.

17

Free Cash Flow to Sales

THE DEFINITION

This definition is similar to margins (discussed in "Magic number" 14 in this book). However, instead of using a range of profit figures as the numerator of the fraction, you use free cash flow instead. This gives a ratio that is a more objective measure of the profitability of a company. In other words, it is free from the effect of any profit "smoothing" that management may be tempted to use.

THE FORMULA

FCF/sales = free cash flow $\times$ 100/sales

THE COMPONENTS

Free cash flow – all cash flow calculations ignore book-entry transactions and concentrate purely on the flows of cash into and out of a business. Hence, they ignore depreciation, amortization of goodwill, retained profits of minority-owned companies, and capitalized interest. As we explained in the previous section, free cash flow also deducts those items that a company cannot avoid paying if it wants to stay in business: interest, tax, and, strictly speaking, sufficient capital spending to maintain its fixed assets. So free cash flow is operating cash flow less interest paid, tax paid, and "maintenance" capital spending.

Annual sales – sales, revenue, or turnover are virtually interchangeable terms and are in such common use as to need little further explanation. Where calculations differ is usually in whether or not you take the sales for the last reported year, or the last 12 months.

Using the last 12 months' figures is common practice for US companies, because they report quarterly. In this case, the figure to take (assuming a forecast is not used) would be the cumulative sales for the preceding four reported quarters. In other words, if a company has recently announced third-quarter sales, the last 12 months' sales figures would be the sales for the nine months of the current year added to the fourth quarter of the previous one.

For companies, like those in the United Kingdom and elsewhere, that report twice yearly, if a half-year has been reported, sales in the first half of the current year would be added to those of the second half of the previous one. Otherwise, the last reported full-year figure would be the correct one to use.

In some respects this is academic. This is because it is sometimes hard to interpret cash flow figures reliably on a half-yearly or quarterly basis, and therefore, for the calculation to be valid and accurate, the "matching" annual sales figure must be used.

WHERE'S THE DATA?

Annual sales – normally this is the topmost figure or subtotal in the consolidated profit and loss account or income statement. Any sales deriving from large one-off business disposals may distort the figure and should, if appropriate, be excluded.

Free cash flow – most of the components of free cash flow (for example, operating cash flow, interest paid, and tax paid) are naturally in the cash flow statement. Avoid confusing the figure for operating cash flow with that of operating profit. Cash flow tables often start with operating profit as the topmost figure, and then show how various adjustments produce operating cash flow.

Capital spending is in the cash flow statement or in the notes relating to it. It is usually under the heading, "net cash outflow for capital expenditure, purchase of fixed assets, and financial investment" – or some combination of these words. Payments for acquisitions (usually termed "purchase of subsidiaries" and the like) and any suspiciously large one-off items can be ignored. Maintenance capital spending is generally assumed to be around one-half or two-thirds of total capital spending.

CALCULATING IT – THE THEORY

Figure 17.1 shows the different numbers to be pulled from the accounts and how to use them to calculate the ratio.

Figure 17.1 Calculating the "Magic Number" for free cash flow to sales

Widget Telecom Pte has the following cash flow and income statement items:

	S$m
Sales	150
Net cash inflow from operations	100
Depreciation	20
Amortization of goodwill	25
Interest paid	−15
Tax paid	−22
Purchases of fixed assets	−17
Sales of fixed assets	2
Free cash flow before capital spend is ...	63
(working)	(100 − 15 − 22)
Maintenance capital spending is ...	−10
(working)	two-thirds (say) of (−17 + 2)
Free cash flow is ...	53
(working)	(63 − 10)
Free cash flow to sales is ...	**35.33%**
(working)	(53 × 100/150)

CALCULATING IT FOR
SINGTEL

Figure 17.2 shows how the highlighted numbers from this extract from the accounts of SingTel combine to produce the "magic number." SingTel is a large pan-Asian telecoms company.

Figure 17.2   Calculating it for SingTel

The figures ...

SingTel's results for the year to March 31, 2003 show the following items:

Group cash flow and capital expenditure

| | Financial year to March 31 | |
| | 2003 | 2002 |
	S$m	S$m
Profit before tax	1,161	2,123
Depreciation	1,730	998
Amortization	633	353
Compensation from IDA	−337	−337
Share of results from associates	−1,032	−241
Exceptional items	819	61
Interest expense	531	270
Adjustment to goodwill	209	0
Other non-cash items	28	−146
Change in working capital	220	342
Dividends from associates	272	67
Tax paid	−461	−460
Free cash flow before capital spending	**3,771**	**3,031**
Capital expenditure	**−1,668**	**−2,999**
Operating revenue	**10,259**	**7,269**

The calculations ...

Free cash flow (company calculation)	2,103	32
(working)	(3,771 − 1,668)	(3,031 − 2,999)
Free cash flow (2/3rd rule)	2,653	1,031
(working)	(3,771 − (0.67 × 1,668))	(3,031 − (0.67 × 2,999))
Free cash flow to sales (company basis)	**20.50%**	**0.44%**
(working)	(2,103 × 100/10,259)	(32 × 100/7,269)
Free cash flow to sales (2/3rd rule)	**25.86%**	**14.18%**
(working)	(2,653 × 100/10,259)	(1,031 × 100/7,269)

As we discovered in the previous section, there are several modes of presentation for cash flow statements, each of which requires a slightly different interpretation. Some US companies reconcile cash flow to profits by taking net income as the basis and then adding back non-cash items. UK companies work the other way round, starting from pre-interest profit and then deducting payments like tax and interest, and adding back book entries like depreciation and amortization.

You need to pay attention to these distinctions because you do not want to deduct tax and interest again, if these deductions are already reflected in the base calculation.

In SingTel's case, in contrast to the example of Microsoft that we used in the previous "magic number," the accounting presentation is straightforward. The company even calculates free cash flow for you, deducting the whole of its capital spending before arriving at free cash flow. This raises a question. Should we use this figure or stick to the estimation method we have used before, taking two-thirds of capital spending as the "maintenance" capital spending figure?

In this instance, because SingTel's network is well established, it might be reasonable to err toward taking the full amount of capital spending as a likely maintenance figure. There is no single right answer in a case like this. What both calculations show is a marked improvement in the figures in the latest reported year over the previous one, and to a much healthier level.

What it Means

Like many other cash flow-based ratios, the importance of the FCF/sales ratio is that it enables companies to be compared irrespective of their size. The concept reduces each company to a common currency. Added to which, of course, cash flow is inherently less susceptible to "smoothing," and therefore gives a truer picture of the company's state of affairs.

The flip side of this is that various factors may conspire to make cash flow per share less predictable than earnings per share, and the growth trend in cash flow may be more erratic than earnings – for reasons that may lie outside the control of the company. This is perhaps particularly true in SingTel's case, because its capital spending appears "lumpy" in the extreme. Other factors contribute to changes in free cash flow, however, including changes to the corporate tax regime and changes from year to year in the timing of receipts and payments.

To repeat, though, the virtue of free cash flow is that it is a more objective measure of the worth of a company, less liable to be "fudged" or "smoothed." To some degree the same is true of sales. Changes in accounting policies, and not least the ingenuity of analysts in manipulating earnings calculations to suit the case they wish to make, do mean profit-based figures can be unreliable. Free cash flow, and ratios based around it, is increasingly being seen as a more reliable means of judging whether or not a company is undervalued or overvalued, and how profitable it is. Even analysts and investment bankers now acknowledge this.

For example, in research published in December 2002 by Morgan Stanley (*European Stock Selection – The Factors That Matter*, p. 3), the firm described changes in FCF/sales and earnings per share growth as, "consistently useful factors for stock selection."

18 Return on Invested Capital

THE DEFINITION

Return on invested capital (ROIC) measures the after-tax cash return a company generates from all of the capital it has invested. Definitions vary slightly. The most widely used definition simply adjusts operating profits for the corporate tax rate and expresses this as a percentage of total capital employed in the business after deducting non-interest-bearing current liabilities.

An alternate definition (cash flow return on invested capital, or CFROIC) uses operating cash flow less tax paid as the numerator.

Either way, comparing this return with the company's cost of capital allows you to work out whether or not the company is adding or destroying value.

THE FORMULAS

CONVENTIONAL DEFINITION

ROIC = (operating income × (1 − corporate tax rate)) × 100/(total assets − non-interest-bearing current liabilities)

ALTERNATE DEFINITION

CFROIC = (operating cash flow − tax paid) × 100/(total assets − non-interest-bearing current liabilities)

THE COMPONENTS

Operating income (or operating profit) – the profit prior to deducting interest and tax, and before crediting any profits from partly owned related companies.

Corporate tax rate – this is found by taking the company tax charge in the income statement and dividing it by pre-tax profit.

Invested capital – the total of all of the assets employed in the business less any non-interest-bearing current liabilities such as trade debtors, income tax, and social security payments. Short-term borrowings are part of invested capital, whereas the standard definition of net capital employed is total assets minus *all* current liabilities.

Operating cash flow less tax paid – this is found in the following way. Take the figure for cash inflow from operations and deduct the tax actually paid by the company in the year in question. This tax figure may be somewhat different from the figure recorded in the income statement. This is because tax relating to one year may be paid in the next or deferred.

WHERE'S THE DATA?

Operating income – in the income statement (profit and loss account), toward the top of the page. Note that operating profit is not the same as gross profit. Operating profit is profit after deducting depreciation and certain other items, but before deducting interest.

Corporate tax rate – the tax figure is found immediately below the pre-tax profit line in the income statement. Divide the tax figure by the pre-tax profit to get the tax rate. This will be a value between zero and one.

Invested capital – take the total of the asset side of the consolidated (or group) balance sheet. Deduct all *non*-interest-bearing current liabilities. These will be in the note to the accounts relating to, "creditors due within one year" or "accounts payable." You need to use judgement to determine the right items to deduct. You can subtract interest-bearing short-term debt from the current liabilities total to get the right amount to deduct from total assets.

Operating cash flow less tax paid – the appropriate figures are easily identifiable in the cash flow statement.

CALCULATING IT – THE THEORY

Figure 18.1 shows the different numbers to be pulled from the accounts that are used to calculate the ratio.

Figure 18.1   Calculating the "Magic Number" for ROIC and CFROIC

Universal Widgets Inc. has the following cash flow, balance sheet, and income statement items:

	$m
Net cash inflow from operations	**100**
Depreciation	20
Amortization of goodwill	25
Interest paid	−15
Tax paid	**−22**
Purchases of fixed assets	−17
Sales of fixed assets	2
Sales	300
Cost of sales	−150
Gross profit	150
Operating costs	−75
Operating profit	75
Interest	−10
Profit before tax	**65**
Taxation	**−20**
Profit after tax	45
Total assets	**250**
Creditors due within one year	
Short-term borrowings	**10**
Current portion of long-term debt	**2**
Trade debtors	12
Social security	3
Tax	15
Dividends	2
Total	**44**

The calculations ...

Invested capital is ...	218
(working)	$(250 - (44 - 10 - 2))$
Corporate tax rate is ...	0.308
(working)	(20/65)
Net operating profit after tax is ...	51.9
(working)	$(75 \times (1 - 0.308))$
ROIC is ...	**23.81%**
(working)	$(51.9 - 100/218)$
After-tax operating cash flow is ...	78
(working)	$(100 - 22)$
CFROIC is ...	**35.78%**
(working)	$(78 \times 100/218)$

CALCULATING IT FOR
SONY

Figure 18.2 shows how the highlighted numbers from this extract from the accounts of Sony combine to produce the "magic number."

Figure 18.2   Calculating it from Sony's 2002 accounts

The figures ...

Year to March 31, 2002	$m
Consolidated statement of cash flows	
Net cash inflow from operations (after deducting tax and interest)	**5,546**
Interest paid	266
Tax paid	**1,114**
Consolidated statements of income	
Sales	56,979
Cost of sales and operating expenses	55,967
Operating profit	1,012
Profit before tax	**698**
Taxation	**490**
Profit after tax	208

Consolidated balance sheet

Total assets	**61,547**

Creditors due within one year

Short-term borrowings	852
Current portion of long-term debt	**1,810**
Trade debtors	5,772
Other accounts payable and accruals	6,538
Tax	793
Deposits from banking customers	**801**
Other	2,671
Total	19,237

The calculations ...

Invested capital is ...		45,773
(working)	$(61,547 - (19,237 - 852 - 1,810 - 801))$	

Total assets are adjusted for current liabilities excluding those that are interest-bearing.

Corporate tax rate is ...		0.702
(working)	(490/698)	

Net operating profit after tax is ...		302
(working)	$(1,012 \times (1 - 0.702))$	

ROIC is ...		**0.66%**
(working)	$(302 \times 100/45,773)$	

After-tax operating cash flow is ...		4,432
(working)	$(5,546 - 1,114)$	

CFROIC is ...		**9.68%**
(working)	$(4,432 \times 100/45,773)$	

The Sony example shows some of the difficulties that can arise when performing the calculation. Like many companies using US accounting principles, Sony compiles its cash flow statement starting from net income after interest and tax, and then making the usual adjustments for non-cash items. We therefore need to add back interest paid to get to the correct numerator for the ROIC and CFROIC calculations. Sony does, however, include the necessary figures in its cash flow statement, so in this instance the calculation is an easy one.

In the balance sheet calculation of invested capital, short-term creditors include deposits of banking customers. By definition these are probably interest-bearing and so must be excluded from non-interest-bearing current liabilities, along with the more normal short-term debt items.

In the income statement we see that Sony has an exceptionally high tax rate, which is almost certainly a temporary aberration. It might be better in this instance to adjust Sony's operating income by a figure such as the average corporate tax rate for Japan and the United States (Sony's main areas of operation). This would produce a less onerous adjustment. Wherever a company's own tax rate varies substantially from the general corporate tax rate, it is worth taking the latter figure as the preferred means of adjustment.

Sony has large non-cash items in its cash flow statement, including around $4.5 billion of depreciation and amortization (including amortization of film costs). This is a good argument for taking the cash-flow return as a better guide to the company's underlying return on invested capital.

WHAT IT MEANS

ROIC and CFROIC are two of the best measures of the real value that is being created by a company's managers for its shareholders and other stakeholders in the business. My personal preference is for the cash flow-based measure, because this is unaffected by accounting quirks and less open to manipulation.

The way you can best gauge shareholder value creation is by comparing CFROIC with weighted average cost of capital (WACC). WACC is a hybrid of cost of equity and cost of debt, weighted by the proportion each contributes to enterprise value. How to calculate WACC was covered in "Magic number" 29 in the original *Magic Numbers* book.

I'll just recap it briefly. Cost of equity is the risk-free rate of return plus the equity risk premium, the combined figure being adjusted for the systemic risk inherent in the equity. In turn, risk is usually represented by 'beta', the volatility of a share relative to the volatility of the market as a whole. Let's look at a simple example.

Say a company has an enterprise value that is comprised of 50 percent equity and 50 percent debt. The risk-free rate of return is 4 percent, the risk premium is 2 percent, the stock's beta is 1.5, and the redemption yield on its debt is 5 percent.

In this example, the cost of equity would be the risk-free rate of return of 4 percent, plus the equity risk premium of 2 percent, making 6 percent, which is then adjusted by the beta of 1.5 to give 9 percent. The WACC would be 7 percent, since each of the two components of the cost of capital in this case (9 percent cost of equity and 5 percent cost of debt) is equally weighted.

Comparing ROIC with WACC is useful, although for fiendishly complicated technical accounting reasons the comparison cannot be an exact one. Nonetheless, you can generally assume that if a company's ROIC is one percentage point or more above its WACC, it will be adding value. The bigger the gap the better it is for you as a shareholder.

Though these ratios take some working out, what they tell you is extremely valuable. Because calculating ROIC and CFROIC is a little more complex than normal, if you persist and accomplish this successfully, it can give you a real edge in predicting the long-term direction of a company's share price. Many investors simply don't bother. Ultimately, you want to own stock in companies that are consistently creating shareholder value, and not own those that aren't doing so.

Be warned! There are plenty of big-name companies that regularly destroy shareholder value through inadequate return on invested capital.

19

Discounted Cash Flow

The Definition

Discounted cash flow (DCF) is a way of valuing companies by forecasting free cash flow for a period of years into the future, and applying a discount factor to each years' figure to reflect the expected time until it accrues. The further in the future, the greater is the discount applied to that year's free cash flow.

The discounted cash flows for each of the future years are then added together. An additional value is placed on the total cash expected to accrue in perpetuity beyond that, and the total of these two items is compared with the current market value of the company to see if its stock is cheap or expensive.

The Formula

DCF = free cash flow year 1 × (d year 1) … etc. … + free cash flow year 10 × (d year 10) + PV of 'perpetuity'.

(d = the discount factor for each year as determined by the chosen discount rate)

Note: DCF calculations can be performed with ease using a standard spreadsheet model.

THE COMPONENTS

Free cash flow – this is operating profit ignoring book-entry transactions. It concentrates purely on the flows of cash into and out of a business. It ignores depreciation, amortization of goodwill, retained profits of minority-owned companies, capitalized interest, and any other items that are merely the result of accounting conventions. Free cash flow also deducts those items that a company cannot avoid paying if it wants to stay in business: interest, tax, and sufficient capital spending to maintain its fixed assets. See the previous sections for more details on how to calculate it.

Forecast growth rates in cash flow – starting from free cash flow for the latest reported year, you need to predict how this figure will grow each year for the next 10 years, or to make a conservative assumption about such growth. This is at your discretion.

"Steady state" growth rate – this is used to calculate the value of the residual cash flow estimated from year 10 onwards. You would normally choose a figure less than the discount rate (see below). A good assumption is to plug in an estimate of the long-term rate of inflation, or assume that today's rate of inflation will hold for the foreseeable future.

Discount rate – this is the rate at which the future cash flows are discounted, each successive year's cash flow reduced by an amount (the discount factor) reflecting the compounded discount rate. The discount factor reflects both investors' preference for cash sooner rather than later, and the greater uncertainty (and vulnerability to subsequent inflation) surrounding cash received in the future. To give a simple example, if the discount rate were 10 percent, year 1 cash flow would be adjusted by multiplying by 100/110, year 2 cash flow would be multiplied by 100/121 to get the discounted figure, year 3 by 100/133.1, and so on.

As a minimum the discount rate should be the risk-free rate of return on 10-year money – reflecting that cash flows are usually predicted and discounted for up to 10 years ahead. To be conservative, you can if you wish add a "risk" premium to the discount rate.

WHERE'S THE DATA?

Free cash flow – you can find operating cash flow and the other adjustments in the cash flow statement. Avoid confusing the figure for operating cash flow with that of operating profit. Cash flow tables often start with operating profit as the topmost figure and then show how the various adjustments produce operating cash flow. See earlier "magic numbers" in this section of the book for more examples of how to calculate it.

Forecast growth rates and "steady state" growth rate – this is estimated by you. Historic growth rates can be used as a guide. The steady state growth rate must be less than the discount rate.

Discount rate – this should be at least the risk-free rate of return on 10-year money, which equates to the yield to maturity on the benchmark 10-year government bond for the country in question. The concept of the risk-free rate of return was covered in the original *Magic Numbers* book.

To this figure you can, if you wish, add an equity risk premium. Data on equity risk premiums are sketchy. The long-term average for the United Kingdom is said to be 5.2 percent. You should probably use a minimum of 2.5–3.0 percent for the least volatile stocks. If the yield on the 10-year bond is, say, 4 percent and the risk premium used is 5 percent, the discount rate used would be 9 percent (4 + 5).

CALCULATING IT – THE THEORY

Figure 19.1 shows the different numbers to be pulled from the accounts and other sources used to calculate the ratio. Fortunately, as we've already mentioned, the whole process can be computerized and the numbers plugged into a relatively simple spreadsheet. This spreadsheet can be downloaded from the web site at *www.magicnumbersbook.com*.

Figure 19.1 Calculating the "Magic Number" for discounted cash flow

Widget Properties is small but rapidly developing. Its DCF spreadsheet looks like this ...

Projected	2003	2004	2005	2006	2007	2008	2009	2010	2011	2012
Prior year cash flow	300	600	900	1,125	1,238	1,361	1,497	1,617	1,714	1,783
Increase %	100.0%	50.0%	25.0%	10.0%	10.0%	10.0%	8.0%	6.0%	4.0%	4.0%
Cash flow	600	900	1,125	1,238	1,361	1,497	1,617	1,714	1,783	1,854
Discounted cash flow	555	770	890	906	921	937	936	918	883	849

Sum of discounted cash flows	8,566
10-year per-share cash flow	£ 0.33
Residual value	
Cash flow in year 10	1,854
Second stage growth rate	2.5%
Cash flow in year 11	1,900
Capitalization	5.6%
Company value at end of year 10	33,814
Present value of future cash flow	22,385
Shares (in thousands)	25,975
Present value per share	**£0.86**

Assumptions and notes

1. Base cash flow calculated as attributable profit (£330,000) plus depreciation and deferred tax less maintenance capex.

2. Discount rate assumed to be the benchmark gilt yield of 4.12% plus a risk premium of 4.0%.

3. The current share price is 30p compared to a net present value of future cash flows of 86p. The shares look cheap if these assumptions are correct.

The figure reproduced here looks slightly different to the downloaded spreadsheet. The spreadsheet file itself contains instructions on how to use it. But remember, that to use this worksheet it is not necessary to fill in any historic figures other than those for the most recent year.

Alternatively, the spreadsheet can be overridden and the free cash flow figure calculated separately and plugged into the top left box of the forecast rows (as shown in the figure). You then enter the projected rates of increases in cash flow for the 10 forward years and for the "second-stage" phase of growth.

These figures can be tailored to take into account any assumptions you might want to make about the timing of growth or decline that is specific to the company, or that might be produced by the impact of the economic cycle. You need also to enter the total number of shares issued, as well as the appropriate discount rate and the current year-end date. The model calculates everything else. The year-end and discount rate used can be changed using the "Entry" tab in the spreadsheet file.

CALCULATING IT FOR
ALTRIA

Figure 19.2 shows how the highlighted numbers from Altria's accounts and various additional assumptions combine to produce the "magic number." Altria, the new name for Philip Morris, is involved in cigarette manufacture in the United States and elsewhere. There is more information on the company at its web site at *www.altia.com*.

Altria's discounted cash flow suggests a value of around $67 for the shares on the assumptions we've used. The price of the shares at the time of writing was around $33 each, suggesting the shares are cheap – if our assumptions are correct.

Figure 19.2 Calculating discounted cash flow for Altria

The figures and calculations ...

Projected	2003	2004	2005	2006	2007	2008	2009	2010	2011	2012
Prior year cash flow	9,266	9,359	9,452	9,547	9,642	9,739	9,836	9,934	10,034	10,134
Increase %	1.0%	1.0%	1.0%	1.0%	1.0%	1.0%	1.0%	1.0%	1.0%	1.0%
Cash flow	9,359	9,452	9,547	9,642	9,739	9,836	9,934	10,034	10,134	10,235
Discounted cash flow	8,775	8,310	7,870	7,453	7,058	6,684	6,330	5,995	5,677	5,376

Sum of discounted cash flows	69,530
10-year per-share cash flow	**34.10**

Residual value

Cash flow in year 10	10,235
Second stage growth rate	0.50%
Cash flow in year 11	10,286
Capitalization	6.15%
Company value at end of year 10	167,255
Present value of future cash flow	136,751
Shares (in millions)	2,039
Present value per share ($)	**67.07**

Assumptions and comments

1. Base year cash flow is as per accounts, deducting 67% of fixed asset purchases as maintenance spending.
2. Discount rate used is 6.65%. This takes the 10-year US dollar swap rate as a proxy and adds a 2.7% equity risk premium.
3. Cash flow is assumed to grow at 1% a year for 10 years and 0.5% thereafter.
4. The current share price is $33.18, which is about half the NPV of discounted cash flows.
5. To equate DCF with the present share price would require a discount rate of 11.30% to be used.

There are several areas where different assumptions could be made. Have we, for example, been too generous in our assumptions about the likely growth in cash flow, bearing in mind the pressure the company may face from possible anti-smoking litigation? Perhaps, but it has been unwise in the past to bet against the ability of cigarette companies to overcome these hurdles and to generate cash regardless. In the end, the assumption about 1 percent per year growth in cash flow for the next decade (and 0.5 percent annually thereafter) seems conservative, bearing in mind the company's past track record.

What about the discount rate? Should we have added a higher equity risk premium to the risk-free rate? Again, this is a matter for judgement, as is the way in which cash flows might fluctuate in the future.

There is another way of interpreting the figures. Use trial and error inputting of different discount rates in the model. By doing this and observing the resulting effect on the present value figure in the model, we can work out the discount rate that exactly equates the total of the discounted cash flows to the current share price. You can then make a judgement as to whether or not this is reasonable.

In the case of Altria, a discount rate of 11.3 percent would be needed to reduce the total of future cash flows sufficiently to equate them to the current share price. A discount rate of 11.3 percent is implying a risk premium over the benchmark rate of more than 7 percent, which seems high, even bearing in mind the risks the company faces from anti-smoking pressure groups and assorted lawyers.

WHAT IT MEANS

Discounted cash flow is a long-established technique originally developed for use by companies assessing capital investment projects. Corporate financiers also use it to work out the true value of companies that are potential bid or buy-out targets.

The technique does, however, involve a lot of subjectivity, not least in assessing future rates of growth. It does, however, have the merit that it is projecting forward from cash flow figures rather than from a set of profit figures. As we have already noted, profits may not tell an accurate story.

Using a market yield as the basis for discount factors is also less subjective than projecting forward from assumptions about likely individual price–earnings ratios and dividend yields. It is also useful in comparing valuations across companies in a relatively stable sector (for example, brewing, tobacco, food retailing, and stores) where similar underlying growth rates can be reasonably confidently assumed. However, there is an element of subjectivity produced in deciding what level of risk premium to add to the underlying discount rate.

The beauty of DCF models is that the figures and assumptions in them can be updated when, for example, new annual accounts are issued, when bond yields and therefore discount factors change, and when other new information comes to light.

The spreadsheet used here is one based on the principles outlined in Robert Hagstrom's book, *The Warren Buffett Way* (Wiley – £17.95). US investment guru Bob Costa devised the spreadsheet. A copy of it is available at *www.magicnumbersbook.com*. To use it you will need Microsoft Excel 5 or higher.

Using DCF models is a good way of getting a handle on whether a particular share represents good value or not. It works less well with cyclical stocks, recovery situations, or companies that do not have a particularly predictable pattern of sales growth.

Part Four

BALANCE SHEET "MAGIC NUMBERS"

BALANCE SHEET "MAGIC NUMBERS"

As we said in the original *Magic Numbers* book, when times are good, many investors pay little attention to the balance sheets of the companies they invest in. As the events of the past two or three years prove, this is a mistake. What looks like a sound company when the weather is fair turns out to be very vulnerable when storm clouds gather.

In liquidation, a company is only worth what people will pay for its assets. And that is often a lot less than you might think they are worth. A company in liquidation is a forced seller, and buyers won't pay over the odds to a forced seller.

Remember, however, that although they are vital to understanding companies, balance sheets take some investigating. Accounting policies vary from company to company. Some of the important information may be buried in the notes to the accounts, and therefore hard to get at.

There are six magic numbers in this section and the final one, the Z-score, is covered in two parts. The first part covers the components of the Z-score calculation and the second the calculation itself. Though complex, a simple spreadsheet can automate the calculation and reduce this complexity. There is a Z-score spreadsheet in the "magic numbers" web site at *www.magicnumbersbook.com*.

Here's a brief rundown of the balance sheet ratios we cover here:

- The current ratio and the acid ratio allow you to examine the short-term resources of the company (or its lack of them).

- Debtor and creditor days let you see how quickly a company is collecting money from its customers, and how fast it is paying its suppliers.

- Stock days tell you how efficient the company is at turning over its stock.

- Gearing tells you how the borrowings of the company compare with its assets, and whether or not the company is vulnerable to changes in interest rates.

- Return on capital shows you how much management is able to generate from all of the capital at its disposal, both equity and debt.

- Each bear market brings an upsurge of interest in the Z-score, a formula designed to highlight a company's strengths and weaknesses. It does this by using ratios not often calculated by conventional investment analysis and combining them in a very specific way.

- The component Z-score ratios are worthy of particular attention, and merit a special "magic number" section of their own

Even more than with some of the earlier numbers, not all of these "magic numbers" are of equal importance in every company, but each is an essential element in the box of tools at investors' disposal.

Debtor and creditor days and stock turnover are critical for businesses that buy and process raw material from outside, or who rely on efficient selling to generate profits. Clearly, debtor days (how fast your customers pay you) are irrelevant for "cash" businesses – since money is handed over immediately.

Gearing is not especially relevant if a company has minimal debt, but should always be investigated anyway.

The Z-score tells you an awful lot about a company's financial soundness and whether or not it might run into trouble in the future. For this reason alone it is worthy of close study, as are its individual component parts.

The sections that follow examine each of these six important balance sheet "magic numbers for stock investors" in more depth. Now read on ...

Current Ratio and "Acid Test" Ratio

THE DEFINITION

These are two closely related ratios that assess a company's short-term liquidity.

The *current ratio* compares current assets (normally stocks, debtors – money owed by customers – and cash) with current liabilities. Current liabilities include bank overdrafts, money the company owes to suppliers and the tax authorities, and other payments that might have to be made at short notice.

The *acid test ratio* (sometimes abbreviated to "acid ratio") is largely the same as the current ratio, but excludes stocks from current assets. This is done because, in an extreme situation, stocks may not be sold for their full price.

The norm to look for in a robust company is that the current ratio is at least 2:1 and the acid ratio at least 1:1. However, as we'll see in the example, this rule does not apply in all cases.

THE FORMULAS

Current ratio = current assets/current liabilities

Acid ratio = (current assets − stocks)/current liabilities

THE COMPONENTS

Current assets – these typically comprise stocks (or inventory), debtors (accounts receivable), and cash. Stocks are defined separately below.

Debtors (accounts receivable, or simply "receivables") – represents the money owed to the company by its customers.

Cash – this item speaks for itself.

Current assets sometimes include short-term investments. To qualify as current assets they must be highly marketable securities (such as short-term government bonds or money market instruments). This means they will vary little in price in the short term and can be quickly sold and turned into cash.

Stocks (sometimes called inventory) – refers to unsold finished goods or those still in the process of being made. The definition sometimes expands, for companies involved in long-term contracts, to include the value of work-in-progress for which customers have not yet been invoiced.

Controlling the level of inventory is vital to a business's health. Stocks represent products that can be turned into cash. Too much stock means that capital is being tied up unnecessarily. For businesses in difficulty, or those selling fashion items, unsold stock may not be as liquid as it appears, or at least not at a "normal" price. To turn it into cash may necessitate deep discounts being offered to tempt buyers.

Current liabilities – in UK accounting parlance such liabilities are "creditors due within one year." In other accounting conventions they may be called "accounts payable." The term is a catch-all for a number of disparate items. These include: short-term bank borrowings and other debt repayable within a year; money owed to suppliers (accounts receivable); liabilities due to government agencies, such as tax payments, VAT, and other items; and dividends to shareholders. Few of these payments can be postponed for long without the company running into trouble.

WHERE'S THE DATA?

Current assets – this item is in the consolidated balance sheet, normally immediately under the items relating to fixed assets. Expanded details of the individual components are normally contained in the notes to the accounts.

Stocks – this is part of the "current assets" group, in the consolidated balance sheet. Expanded details on stocks (inventory) may also be in the note to the accounts relating to current assets. A guide to the way in which the stock values have been reached may also be in the note about significant accounting policies.

Current liabilities – these are also in the consolidated balance sheet, normally immediately below the current assets item. The term "current liabilities" may be used, or "short-term creditors," or "creditors due within one year."

CALCULATING IT – THE THEORY

Figure 20.1 shows the different numbers to be pulled from the accounts and how to use them to calculate the ratio.

Figure 20.1   Calculating the "Magic Number" for current ratio and acid ratio

Consolidated Flanges plc has current assets and current liabilities that look like this:

	£m
Current assets	
Stocks	20
Debtors	15
Cash	10
Total	**45**
Current liabilities	
Short-term borrowing	5
Trade creditors	14
Other current liabilities	11
Total	**30**
The current ratio is ...	**1.5**
(working)	(45/30)
The acid ratio is ...	**0.83**
(working)	(45 − 20)/30

CALCULATING IT FOR
McDONALD'S

Figure 20.2 shows how the highlighted numbers from this extract from the accounts of McDonald's combine to produce the "magic number." More information is available at the company's web site at *www.mcdonalds.com*. McDonald's is a US-based global fast food restaurant chain. It serves 43 million people a day in 120 countries.

Figure 20.2   Calculating it for McDonald's

The figures ...

2002 Financial Report

	$m
Current assets	
Cash and equivalents	330.4
Accounts and notes receivable	855.3
Inventories (at lower of cost or market)	**111.7**
Prepayments and other	418.0
Total	**1,715.40**
Current liabilities	
Notes payable	0.3
Accounts payable	635.8
Income taxes	16.3
Other taxes	191.8
Accrued interest	199.4
Accrued restructuring charges	328.5
Accrued payroll and other liabilities	774.7
Current maturities of long-term debt	275.5
Total	**2,422.30**

The current ratio is ...	**0.71**
(working)	(1,715.4/2,422.3)

The acid ratio is ...	**0.66**
(working)	((1,715.4 − 111.7)/2,422.3)

The calculation here is straightforward. Stocks ("inventories") are stated clearly in the accounts and there are no other complications.

WHAT IT MEANS

Investors may feel more comfortable with a company that has a liquid balance sheet (plenty of cash and current assets well in excess of current liabilities). But there are plenty of good companies that do not conform to this model. McDonald's falls into this category. Whether or not a low current ratio and low acid ratio is a cause for concern depends on the nature of the business, the company's own market position, and the salability or otherwise of its stocks.

McDonald's in fact illustrates the exception to the general rule about "normal" current ratios being 2:1 and acid ratios being 1:1 or more. This is the case of companies that operate in cash businesses and that can dominate their suppliers. A good example here is that of UK supermarket groups. These take cash from customers on a daily basis, but, because of their buying power, enjoy useful credit terms from suppliers, whom they may pay on, say, a monthly basis. McDonald's falls into exactly the same category, as does a company like Starbucks, or any other high street cash business.

In these instances, the business might have what seems to be a relatively illiquid "current" balance sheet and a low acid ratio, but nonetheless be perfectly sound. The company's influence in the market allows it to use its suppliers as sources of short-term working capital.

What is good for global fast food chains, supermarkets, and large multinationals is less good for struggling small companies producing specialized products. This is where these ratios really come into play. In this instance, stocks may be hard to liquidate and the company may have little pricing power or effective credit control over customers and little opportunity to influence suppliers' terms.

One final point. Companies generally choose the most favorable point in the year to have their year-end. Generally, that is when assets and cash are at their maximum and debts and liabilities are at their lowest. For example, US and European retailers generally choose January year-ends. This is because at that time of year their balance sheets are full of cash after the Christmas and New Year holiday seasons. There is no harm in this, just so long as you realize that the balance sheet ratios you calculate are usually taken at a point that is as good as it gets.

21 Debtor Days and Creditor Days

THE DEFINITION

The previous "magic number" gave an insight into the way current assets and liabilities are made up. Debtors and creditors are an important part of the balance sheet, too. Debtors (accounts receivable) represent money owed to the company by customers. Creditors (accounts payable) are unpaid bills the company owes to suppliers and others. *Creditor days* and *debtor days* are a way of relating these figures to the company's turnover. They measure how quickly the company is paying its bills, and how quickly its customers are paying up.

THE FORMULAS

Debtor days = (trade debtors × 365)/sales

Creditor days = (trade creditors × 365)/cost of sales

In other words, the ratios are the proportion that year-end trade debtors or creditors represent of annual sales or cost of sales, expressed in days.

THE COMPONENTS

Trade debtors (accounts receivable, or "receivables") – invoiced sales that have not been paid at the balance sheet date. It is important to distinguish between debtors as a whole and trade debtors in particular, although the two figures will sometimes be the same. Trade debtors are used in the calculation.

Trade creditors (accounts payable) – bills for goods and services purchased from suppliers that have not been paid for at the balance sheet date. It is important to distinguish between trade creditors and other creditors, such as tax and social security, VAT and other sales, and so on, which typically have fixed payment periods outside the company's control. These are normally excluded from the calculation of creditor days.

Annual sales – sales, revenue, or turnover are virtually interchangeable terms and are in such common use as to need little further explanation. In the case of calculating debtor days, the sales figure taken should be the one for the year to which the balance sheet debtors and creditors also relate. Debtor days are in effect the proportion of annual sales, which customers had not paid for at the end of the year.

Cost of sales – this is the amount subtracted from sales to arrive at gross profit. The figure comprises the cost of materials, goods, and services the company has to buy from outside. This figure is used as part of the calculation of creditor days, because trade creditors represent the proportion of these bills that are unpaid at the year-end. As with the corresponding sales figure, this item should also be the one for the year/year-end to which the creditors relate.

WHERE'S THE DATA?

Trade debtors – this is in the notes to the accounts referred to from the current assets side of the consolidated balance sheet. Occasionally, trade debtors are stated on the face of the balance sheet itself.

Trade creditors – this is in the notes to the accounts referred to from the current liabilities ("creditors due within one year") item in the consolidated balance sheet. Occasionally, trade creditors will be stated on the face of the balance sheet.

Annual sales – normally this is the topmost figure or subtotal in the consolidated profit and loss account or income statement. The total sales figure should be taken.

Cost of sales – this is normally the item immediately below the sales total and above the gross profit figure in the income statement of the profit and loss account.

CALCULATING IT – THE THEORY

Figure 21.1 shows the different numbers to be pulled from the accounts and how to use them to calculate the ratio.

Figure 21.1   Calculating the "Magic Number" for debtor days and creditor days

Singapore Widgets Pte has ...	
	S$m
Sales of ...	100
Cost of sales of ...	80
Trade debtors of ...	25
Trade creditors of ...	18
Debtor days are ... (working)	**91 days** (25 × 365/100)
Creditor days are ... (working)	**82 days** (18 × 365/80)

CALCULATING IT FOR
WPP

Figure 21.2 shows how the numbers selected from the 2002 accounts of WPP combine to produce the "magic numbers." WPP is a global advertising and marketing services company. More information about the company is at *www.wpp.com*.

Figure 21.2 Calculating it for WPP's 2002 accounts

The figures ...

Year to December 31 (£m)	2002	2001
From income statement ...		
Sales (gross billings) are ...	18,029	20,887
Cost of sales is ...	14,120	16,865
From group balance sheet and related notes		
Trade debtors inside WC facility ...	168	249
Trade debtors outside WC facility ...	1,753	1,841
Trade creditors are ...	2,478	2,506

The figures are easily identifiable from within the accounts and the notes, and have been rounded to make calculation simpler.

The calculations ...

	2002	2001
Debtor days are ...	**39 days**	**37 days**
(working)	$(168 + 1,753) \times 365/18,029$	$(249 + 1,841) \times 365/20,887$
Creditor days are ...	**64 days**	**54 days**
(working)	$(2,478 \times 365/14,120)$	$(2,506 \times 365/16,865)$

WPP collects on invoices to clients in 39 days and pays its suppliers in 64 days.

The example demonstrates some of the problems involved in calculating these figures. You need to think about the nature of the business to calculate the numbers properly.

In the case of WPP, sales and cost of sales, and debtors and creditors, are big numbers relative to pre-tax profits and net income. WPP had total sales of £18 billion in 2002, but its pre-tax income was only £205 million. The company did not have a stellar year in 2002, but one reason why the numbers are so far apart is that the company includes, in its client billings, a large number of third-party costs. These are passed on direct to clients. They include items such as the cost of TV airtime or advertising space in newspapers. WPP's own internally generated revenue – the money that clients are actually paying the company for the provision of its services – is only £3.91 billion.

This means that debtor and creditor days are crucial ratios for WPP because the billings involved are large relative to the company's profits. In the example, the ratios show that in round terms the company collects its own fees (and payments due to third parties like newspapers and broadcasters) from its clients in around 40 days, keeps the third-party fees for a couple of weeks, and then pays the suppliers.

So long as there is a lag between payments coming in from clients and payments going out to suppliers, the company does not have to find additional capital. In fact, it can earn interest on the payments due for a couple of weeks. Because of the size of the numbers involved, the company has a special working capital facility from its bankers – a "float" – to allow it to smooth out any temporary leads and lags in payments and receipts.

What they Mean

Together with stock days (see the next "magic number"), debtor and creditor days are a crucial link between the company's income statement, its balance sheet, and its cash flow. While in the income statement a company can book sales and profits, if it is slower than before at collecting its bills and suppliers demand faster payment, then cash receipts will not reflect the trend in profits.

As with some other ratios, the absolute level of debtor and creditor days is less important than the trend over time and how the company compares with its competitors.

Different industries collect and pay bills at different speeds, depending on the inherent nature of the business. But if a company's performance in this area is inferior to its competitors (that is, it collects its overdue invoices slower and is forced to pay its own debts faster), it is a sign of weakness. Similarly, deterioration in credit control over time is a worrying trend.

Not all companies are susceptible to this analysis. Creditor days are not meaningful where the company's bought-in cost of sales is low and the company generates most value internally. Asset-based companies and those with long-term contracts may not be suitable cases for analysis. Here, more attention should be focused on the length of the company's order book relative to its turnover, and on how revenue from long-term contracts is booked.

22 Stock Days and Stockturn

THE DEFINITION

Stock days relate the level of a company's stocks to its annual sales and express the result as a number of days. This ratio is sometimes called *stockturn*. This is expressed as a multiple: the number of times stock turns over in the course of a year.

THE FORMULAS

Stock days = stocks × 365/sales

Stock turn = sales/stocks

If expressed in the form of stock days, a lower number of days indicate greater efficiency. If expressed as stockturn, the higher the figure the better, since this indicates faster turnover of stock and hence greater efficiency.

THE COMPONENTS

Stocks (or inventory) – these are stocks of finished goods that have not been sold, or a work-in-progress that has not yet been completed. In the case of manufacturing companies, stocks are the result of the company's own production. In the case of retailers, stocks are goods purchased from suppliers but not yet been sold.

Annual sales – sales, revenue, or turnover are virtually interchangeable terms. They are in such common use as to need little further explanation. In the case of calculating stock days or stockturn, the sales figure taken should be the one for the year and year-end to which the balance sheet stock figure relates.

WHERE'S THE DATA?

Stocks (or inventory) – this is found in the consolidated (or group) balance sheet in current assets.

Annual sales – this is normally the topmost figure or subtotal in the consolidated profit and loss account or income statement. The total sales figure should be taken.

CALCULATING IT – THE THEORY

Figure 22.1 shows the different numbers to be pulled from the accounts and how to use them to calculate the ratio.

Figure 22.1   Calculating the "Magic Number" for stock days and stockturn

Freedom Widgets Inc. has …

Annual sales of …	$600m
Stocks (or inventory) of …	$183m
Stock days are …	**111 days**
(working)	(183 × 365/600)

Widget Retail Inc. has …

Annual sales of …	$3,657m
Stocks (or inventory) of …	$457m
Stockturn is …	**8 times**
(working)	(3,657/457)

Stock and stock days are mirror images of each other. Stockturn can be converted into stock days by dividing it into 365. Similarly, dividing 365 by stock days produces stockturn.

Figure 22.2 shows how the highlighted numbers from this extract from the fiscal 2002 accounts of the multinational film and electronics giant Sony (see *www.sony.com* for more information) combine to produce the "magic number."

Figure 22.2 Calculating stockturn and stock days for Sony

The figures ...

Year to March (figures in Ybn)	2002	2001
Annual sales of ...	7,578	7,314
Stocks (or inventory) of ...	673	943
Stock days are ...	**32 days**	**47 days**
(working)	(673 × 365/7,578)	(943 × 365/7,314)
Stockturn is ...	**11.4 times**	**7.8 times**
(working)	(365/32)	(365/47)

Dividing stock days into 365 produces stockturn – the number of times stock turns over in the course of a year.

Although the calculation for Sony itself is fairly straightforward, in the case of some companies, you may have to make decisions about what precisely to include or exclude, especially in respect of turnover.

Should you exclude, for example, sales relating to businesses acquired during the year? Strictly speaking, to get a wholly accurate figure the answer is "yes." In practice, it is next to impossible to do this. Stocks attributable to an acquired business cannot be separated from the overall stock figure, and hence taking the global figure is the only correct course of action.

Some companies also have joint ventures. In this case, each "parent" company balance sheet only includes its share of net assets. Stock figures are not usually given separately. In this case, taking turnover excluding sales attributable to joint ventures is, in the absence of any better information, the right course of action.

WHAT IT MEANS

Debtor days, creditor days, and stock days or stockturn are sometimes called working capital ratios. They measure the degree to which management is minimizing the amount of day-to-day capital tied up in the form of unsold stocks, uncollected invoices, or unpaid bills.

As with debtor and creditor days, different industries have different stock cycles. These relate to differences in manufacturing processes or, in the case of retailers, to the differing types of goods they sell. In Sony's case we have a business that has operations in consumer electronics, computer games, music, film, and financial services, all of which have different operating characteristics.

Like most companies, Sony analyzes its revenue between divisions, but not its inventory figure, so the stock days figure calculated in the example in Figure 22.2 is an amalgam of the different stock cycles for all of these businesses. It doesn't take rocket science to realize that this has some limitations.

In Sony's case, however, what we can say is that the figure improved over the years covered in the example. That's to say the company turned its stock over faster. But whether the improvement was uniform or simply related to one or two parts of the company's business is hard to gauge.

As with debtor and creditor days, what also matters more with stock days and stockturn is the trend in the ratio rather than its absolute level. Companies in broadly similar businesses should be measured against the ratios achieved by the most efficient company in the industry to see how they stack up.

Remember too that stock days or stockturn is of no help in assessing a business that does not normally have stock as part of its day-to-day business. Software or intellectual property licensing businesses, bookmakers, and casinos are just some of the examples where it is of little use. Sony, for instance, has a mixture of businesses, some of which have a heavy element of intellectual capital involved. It's another reason for being slightly wary of drawing too many conclusions from this one number.

23

Gearing

THE DEFINITION

Gearing, sometimes called the debt–equity ratio, is usually defined as net borrowings (that's to say total borrowings minus cash) divided by tangible shareholders' equity, with the result expressed as a percentage.

An alternate definition is net borrowings divided by tangible shareholders' equity plus net debt, with the result expressed as a percentage.

THE FORMULAS

Gearing 1 = (total borrowings − cash) × 100/tangible shareholders' equity

Gearing 2 = net debt × 100/(tangible shareholders' equity + net debt)

THE COMPONENTS

Total borrowings – this is the sum of all items representing borrowed money or debt securities. It can include both short-term and long-term items. Typically, it takes in bank borrowings and overdrafts, the current portion of long-term debt, medium and long-term bank borrowings, and currently outstanding bond issues.

Cash – needs little further explanation, except to say that in addition to bank cash it is also sometimes acceptable to add in short-term investments that are near to cash in their characteristics. This means they are easily saleable and not subject to anything other than vary small movements in value. Examples of this "near cash" are very short-term government bonds and certificates of deposit.

Shareholders' equity – this goes by a number of different names, including book value, stockholders' or shareholders' equity, shareholders' funds, net assets, and net tangible assets. Whatever the terminology, it represents the tangible fixed assets of the business plus current assets, less current liabilities, long-term creditors, and provisions. The difference between these numbers represents the residual assets that are "owned" by shareholders.

The alternative way of calculating this figure is to take the total of share capital and reserves, and deduct any intangible assets – the value of trademarks or brand names, customer lists, or simply the goodwill paid when another business is acquired.

Goodwill is the amount paid for a business in excess of its asset value. Intangible assets are usually separately identified in the balance sheet.

WHERE'S THE DATA?

Total borrowings – the items that make up this number are located in different parts of the balance sheet. Short-term borrowings are in current liabilities (sometimes called "creditors due within one year"). They are variously identified as bank borrowings, overdrafts, and/or the current portion of long-term debt. Long-term borrowings are normally stated separately, or as part of long-term creditors. You may need to add four or five figures together to produce a figure for total borrowings. Borrowings are sometimes assembled in a single note to the accounts, which may simplify their identification and act as a cross-check.

Cash – this is in current assets, as a separate and distinct item. It may also be necessary to include some or all of a figure for short-term investments, found in the same place. There is usually some explanation about the nature of the investments and how they are valued in the relevant note. You can use this to decide whether or not they should be included in cash.

Shareholders' equity – this is found on the face of the consolidated balance sheet normally using one of the alternative phrases listed earlier. It is also often represented by, and identifiable as, the total of share capital and various different reserves. As noted previously, intangible assets should be deducted from this figure when calculating gearing.

CALCULATING IT – THE THEORY

Figure 23.1 shows the different numbers to be pulled from the accounts and how to use them to calculate the ratio.

Figure 23.1   Calculating the "Magic Number" for gearing

Tokyo Microwidgets has the following items in its balance sheet:

	¥bn
Intangible assets	40
Cash	15
Short-term government bonds	5
Bank overdrafts	35
Current portion of long-term debt	25
Long-term borrowings	20
2% bond 2010	100
Ordinary share capital	20
Capital reserves	200
Revenue reserves	300
Total share capital and reserves	520

Working from the numbers to build up the components of the ratio ...

Tangible shareholders' equity is ... (working)	480 (520 − 40)
Cash is ... (working)	20 (15 + 5)
Total borrowings are ... (working)	180 (35 + 25 + 20 + 100)
Gearing 1 is ... (working)	**33.33%** (180 − 20) × 100/480
Gearing 2 is ... (working)	**25.00%** (180 − 20) × 100/(480 + (180 − 20))

Figure 23.2 shows how the highlighted numbers from this extract from the accounts of SingTel combine to produce the "magic number." SingTel (its web address is *www.singtel.com*) is a Singapore company providing pan-Asian telecommunications.

Figure 23.2   Calculating gearing from SingTel's 2003 accounts

The figures ...

Group Balance Sheets as at March 31	2003 S$m	2002 S$m
Share capital	2,674	2,674
Reserves	12,796	11,905
Share capital and reserves	**15,470**	**14,579**
Minority interests	149	453
Intangible assets and goodwill (incl. above)	**10,816**	**11,570**
Current Assets		
Short-term investments	**108**	515
Cash and bank balances	**949**	1,729
Current liabilities		
Borrowings (secured)	**340**	98
Borrowings (unsecured)	**428**	295
Non-current liabilities		
Borrowings (secured)	**958**	1,079
Borrowings (unsecured)	**8,946**	10,405

The calculations ...

Gearing 1 (excluding goodwill) is ...   206.60%
(working) $(8,946 + 958 + 340 + 428 - 108 - 949) \times 100/(15,470 - 10,816)$

Gearing 1 (including goodwill) is ...   62.15%
(working) $(8,946 + 958 + 340 + 428 - 108 - 949) \times 100/15,470$

Gearing 2 is ...   67.38%
(working) $(8,946 + 958 + 340 + 428 - 108 - 949) \times 100/15,470 - 10,816$
             $+ (8,946 + 958 + 340 + 428 - 108 - 949)$

Net debt multiplied by 100 divided by net tangible assets plus net debt. The calculation is in fact $9,615 \times 100/4,654 + 9,615$.

When we used it as the example for the gearing calculation in the original *Magic Numbers* book, we noted that Singtel's net cash represented some 65 percent of shareholders' equity. This meant that the company at that time had "gearing in reverse." We commented that "SingTel is liquid, but this may mean it has an acquisition in view."

This proved to be the case. SingTel acquired Optus, an Australian-based telecoms business, from Cable & Wireless, completing the acquisition in October 2001. While gearing has obviously changed markedly since our original example, the numbers in Figure 22.2 require no particular adjustment. The current gearing figure and that of the prior year are truly comparable, since both years would have included the full balance sheet effect of the acquisition in the subsequent March 31, 2002 and March 31, 2003 year-end accounts.

The example does show, however, how different methods of calculation affect the resulting gearing figure. In SingTel's case, excluding intangible assets and goodwill makes the biggest difference to the calculation. Our view is that these items should be excluded, since they reflect in large measure what SingTel has paid for acquisitions in excess of their book value. They may or may not have been the correct course of action. Even if they were, the goodwill figure should not be allowed to bury their true balance sheet consequences.

Companies should be able to stand being compared on the basis of the strictest definition of gearing, which in SingTel's case is more than 2:1. On the more loosely defined calculations, gearing drops to between 60 percent and 70 percent. SingTel's own accounts show gearing at 38 percent. This is a figure arrived at by taking debt as a percentage of shareholders' funds, including intangibles and goodwill, minorities and net debt, which is about as broad a definition as you can get.

WHAT IT MEANS

Gearing provokes more debate than almost any other financial ratio. Like many other "magic numbers," it is the context that is important. Is the gearing ratio significantly higher than the company's major competitors? Is the underlying business stable? Does it generate reliable flows of cash? In SingTel's case, for example, though the company may have high gearing based on conventional calculations, it also has very strong cash generation, too.

Other questions include whether or not the valuations of the company's assets are up to date, whether or not interest rates are moving up or down, how much debt is at variable rates of interest, and whether all of the cash is readily available to the company.

All these factors are important. A high gearing ratio may simply be an indicator that assets are undervalued. If so, the true shareholders' equity figure is higher than the balance sheet might indicate, and gearing overstated. Companies with stable reliable cash flow, like SingTel, can support higher levels of gearing than those in more volatile businesses.

If profits are rising, high gearing can enhance profit growth and returns to equity shareholders. Other things being equal, the profits of highly geared companies can benefit if interest rates are falling, or if the debt is paying interest at variable rates.

Equally, assets can be overvalued and gearing therefore understated, high gearing will exaggerate falling profits, and highly geared companies may suffer if interest rates rise.

Financial theory suggests that investors should be indifferent to a company's capital structure, provided that the company is minimizing its cost of capital. However, in the real world, gearing does, if nothing else, affect investor sentiment. When times are tough, highly geared companies are seen as vulnerable. They may see their stock market rating and credit ratings suffer, and find it harder and more costly to borrow.

24 Return on Capital Employed

THE DEFINITION

Return on capital employed (ROCE) is one of several ratios that compare profits made to assets used in the business. Return on capital is the percentage that profit before interest and tax represents of net capital employed.

Net capital employed (NCE) is the capital provided for use in the business by equity shareholders, and by other long-term creditors and providers of capital such as bondholders.

ROCE is often calculated as the average of opening and closing capital employed. You do this because it is the capital employed during the year (not at the year-end) that generates the return. If calculated this way, the ratio is called return on average capital employed (ROACE).

THE FORMULAS

ROCE = PBIT $\times$ 100/net capital employed (NCE)

ROACE = PBIT $\times$ 100/(NCE at prior year end + NCE at latest year end)/2

THE COMPONENTS

Net capital employed – this is the capital provided for use in the business by equity shareholders and other long-term creditors and providers of capital such as bondholders. You can work it out quite simply by taking the total of all balance sheet assets and deducting current liabilities. Current liabilities are excluded because they are not capital that is permanently available.

Average capital employed – this is the net capital employed at the beginning of the year (in effect the net capital employed figure for the prior year-end) plus the net capital employed at the end of the year, with the total divided by two to produce the average.

PBIT – profit before interest and tax is calculated simply by adding back the interest charge to the pre-tax profit figure.

WHERE'S THE DATA?

Net capital employed – this is often given as a separate item in the consolidated or group balance sheet, usually about halfway down the page. If the figure is not given, total assets should be clearly visible and current liabilities (creditors due within one year) should be deducted from total assets to arrive at net capital employed. Most accounts contain at least two years of data, so you can calculate opening capital employed by using the same data for the prior year.

Profit before interest and tax – this is in the income statement or profit and loss account. Pre-tax profit and the interest charge can usually be easily identified without recourse to the notes. Remember, however, that if the company has net interest earned rather than net interest paid (that is, if the company has net cash rather than net borrowings), PBIT will be smaller than the pre-tax profit figure.

CALCULATING IT – THE THEORY

Figure 24.1 shows the different numbers to be pulled from the accounts and how to use them to calculate the ratio.

Figure 24.1 Calculating the "Magic Number" for return on capital

Aussie Widgets has relevant profit and loss and balance sheet numbers as follows:

	2003 A$m	2002 A$m
Operating profit	20	18
Associated companies	5	4
less Interest paid	3	3
Pre-tax profit	22	19
Intangible assets	15	15
Fixed assets	150	145
Current assets	25	20
Total assets	190	180
Creditors – due within one year	30	26
Pre-interest profit is ...	25	22
(working)	(22 + 3)	(19 + 3)
Net capital employed is ...	160	154
(working)	(190 − 30)	(180 − 26)
Average capital employed is ...	157	
(working)	(160 + 154)/2	
Return on capital employed is ...	**15.63%**	
(working)	(25 × 100)/160	
Return on average capital employed is ...	**15.92%**	
(working)	(25 × 100)/157	

Note that average capital employed for 2002 cannot be calculated without the year-end 2001 figures.

Figure 24.2 shows how the highlighted numbers from this extract from the accounts of GE combine to produce the "magic number." GE is a leading US industrial holding company with businesses in a range of industries, including financial services, aero engines, broadcasting, and consumer products. More information on the company is at *www.ge.com.*

Figure 24.2   Calculating the "Magic Number" from GE's 2002 accounts

The figures ...

Income statement	2002 $m	2001 $m
Earnings before income taxes	18,891	19,701
Interest and financial charges (previously deducted)	10,216	11,062
Consolidated balance sheet		
Intangible assets	46,180	35,124
Total assets	575,244	495,023
Current liabilities	181,827	198,904
Pre-interest profit is ... (working)	29,107 (18,891 + 10,216)	30,763 (19,701 + 11,062)
Net capital employed is ... (working)	393,417 (575,244 − 181,827)	296,119 (495,023 − 198,904)
Average capital employed is ... (working)	344,768 (393,417 + 296,119)/2	
Return on capital employed is ... (working)	**7.40%** (29,107 × 100)/393,417	
Return on average capital employed is ... (working)	**8.44%** (29,107 × 100)/344,768	

Note that average capital employed for 2001 cannot be calculated without the year-end 2000 figures.

GE's return on capital is undeniably low at present, although you could argue the case for excluding intangibles from the calculation. We prefer not to, since the cash spent on acquisitions in excess of book value, the way goodwill and intangible assets are created, is still cash that has been spent on shareholders' behalf and ought to earn a return.

WHAT IT MEANS

It is easy to get confused between different return figures, and differences between them can be given an importance that is not warranted. Good companies have high returns on capital: bad ones often have low ones. But even this distinction is not absolute. Cyclical stocks – GE has a number of cyclical businesses, for example – can show sharply fluctuating levels of profitability. Buy them at the right point in the cycle and they will be profitable investments, even though their returns may look low.

Return on capital does not distinguish between the different types of capital on which the return is earned; it simply measures the return generated by the company on the capital irrespective of its source or cost.

Measuring ROCE against cost of capital can be revealing. But in this case you need to work out the return using an after-tax version of PBIT. This is usually called NOPLAT (net operating profits less adjusted taxes). We covered a version of this type of calculation in "Magic number" 18, which looked at return on invested capital and cash flow return on invested capital.

Why is return on capital and return on invested capital so important? The reason that companies perform poorly against their peers is usually down to inefficient management of assets – too many under-performing peripheral businesses – or else to factors outside the company's control, perhaps a tough regulatory regime.

Set these returns against the companies' cost of capital and you can really make a definitive comparison. Unless a company makes a return significantly over and above its cost of capital it is in effect gradually destroying the capital base of the business. Shareholders are the ultimate victims of this process. This makes ROCE (and ROIC – covered earlier) a vital measuring gauge.

In GE's case, its cost of capital is probably fairly low, so it would be hard to argue that it is consistently destroying shareholder value. The performance of the shares over very many years attests otherwise.

Z-Score Components

THE DEFINITION

The Z-score is a method of gauging the financial standing of a company – that's to say, whether or not it is likely to fail in the short or medium term. It takes a number of key ratios – part income statement and part balance sheet – and combines them in a unique formula of its own.

The ratios in question are: working capital/total assets; retained earnings/total assets; EBIT/total assets; market capitalization/total liabilities; and sales to total assets.

THE FORMULAS

WC/TA = (stocks + debtors − short-term creditors)/total assets

RE/TA = accumulated retained earnings/total assets

EBIT/TA = (PBT + interest paid − interest received)/total assets

MC/TL = (year-end shares in issue × share price)/total liabilities

S/TA = sales/total assets

THE COMPONENTS

Working capital (WC) – there are various ways of interpreting working capital. One would be to take stocks and trade debtors and deduct trade creditors. Another might be to take stocks and add in all accounts receivable (another name for debtors) and deduct all accounts payable (another name for creditors). A third way would be to include the balance of net short-term debt or cash as part of working capital. In this particular definition, we take stocks plus accounts receivable, minus accounts payable.

Retained earnings (RE) – in this context, retained earnings is a balance sheet reserve. It represents the accumulated amounts retained by the company since its inception and is sometimes known by the term profit and loss account reserve. It is *not* the retained earnings figure quoted in the income, but the accumulation of those figures over many years.

EBIT – this item is defined as earnings (or profit) before interest and tax. The best way to calculate this is to take profit before tax, deduct any interest income and add any interest expense. The significance of this item is that it allows companies to be compared in profit terms irrespective of how little or how much debt or cash they carry in their balance sheet.

Market capitalization (MC) – a company's total shares in issue multiplied by its share price. This is a standard measure of the stock market value of a company and is used in a variety of ways. This was "Magic number" 1 in the original *Magic Numbers* books.

Sales (S) – sales, revenue, or turnover are virtually interchangeable terms. They are in such common use as to need little further explanation. Where calculations differ is in whether or not, in performing this calculation, you take the sales for the last reported year, or the last 12 months. In this instance we need to use the annual sales for the last reported year.

Total assets (TA) – this is the total of all assets, including fixed assets, investments, and current assets. It is a moot point whether or not intangible assets should be included. The inclusion of intangible assets reduces the Z-score. To be conservative therefore, intangible assets *should* be counted as part of total assets. It is also important to distinguish between total assets and net capital employed (NCE), which is a different figure. NCE is total assets less current liabilities.

Total liabilities (TL) – this is the total of short-term creditors, long-term creditors, and provisions for liabilities and charges. As an aside, total assets less total liabilities equate to shareholders' equity, the residual owned pro-rata by those who hold shares in the company.

WHERE'S THE DATA?

Annual sales – this is normally the topmost figure or subtotal in the consolidated profit and loss account or income statement. Any sales deriving from large one-off business disposals may distort the figure and should, if appropriate, be excluded.

Retained earnings – this is in the balance sheet under the heading shareholders' or stockholders' equity, sometimes called share capital and reserves. Look for the item headed "retained earnings" or "profit and loss account."

Issued shares outstanding (for calculating market capitalization) – this is in the notes to the accounts. The note can be found from a reference in the consolidated balance sheet next to the heading, "called-up share capital" or a similar term. The number of ordinary shares at the end of the year should be taken, and not their stated nominal money value (if any).

Share (stock) price (for calculating market capitalization) – found in any daily newspaper or financial web site. Take care to use the actual share price and not the prices of any options, warrants, partly paid shares, or other derivatives. Take note also of the units in which the share price is expressed. In the United Kingdom, shares are traditionally quoted in pence, but in $ in the United States and in € in Continental Europe.

Balance sheet items – all other balance sheet items will be found on the face of the consolidated (sometimes called group) balance sheet.

In the case of working capital, stocks and debtors are found under the current assets heading, and creditors due within one year under current liabilities.

Items relating to cash, current investments, and short-term borrowings should be excluded.

Total assets are the sum of fixed assets and all current assets.

Total liabilities are the sum of creditors due within one year, other creditors, and provisions for liabilities and charges.

As a cross-check, total assets minus total liabilities should equal the total of share capital and reserves.

CALCULATING THEM — THE THEORY

Figure 25.1 shows the different numbers to be pulled from the accounts and how to use them to calculate these ratios.

Figure 25.1 Calculating the "Magic Number" for Z-score components

Bonza Pharma Pty Ltd, an Australian drug company, has the following income statement, balance sheet, and share price numbers:

Profit and loss account

Year to December 31	2002 A$m	2001 A$m
Sales	**1,000**	**950**
Cost of sales	800	775
Gross profit	200	175
Total operating expenses	120	100
Profit before interest and tax	**80**	**75**
Less Interest	10	10
Profit before tax	70	65
less Tax	20	18
Net profit attributable	50	47
Ordinary dividends	10	10
Retained earnings	40	37

Balance sheet

As at December 31	2002 A$m	2001 A$m
Intangible assets	500	500
Tangible fixed assets	1,000	1,000
Current assets		
Stocks	**50**	**45**
Debtors	**45**	**40**
Cash	80	100
Total	175	185
Total assets	**1,675**	**1,685**

Creditors due within one year	30	45
Short-term borrowings	100	100
Long-term borrowing	150	150
Long-term creditors	20	20
Provisions for liabilities and charges	300	200
Total liabilities	**600**	**515**
Stockholders' equity	1,075	1,180
Including reserve for retained earnings	**450**	**445**
Shares in issue	**150m**	**150m**
Share price	**A$6.00**	

The basic parameters required for the calculations are (note numbers highlighted above):

Sales	1,000	950
EBIT	80	75
Working capital	65	40
(working)	(50 + 45 − 30)	(45 + 40 − 45)
Total assets	1,675	1,685
Reserve for retained earnings	450	445
Total liabilities	600	515
Market capitalization	A$900m	
(working)	(150 × 6)	

The ratios are:

Working capital/total assets	**0.039**	**0.024**
(working)	(65/1,675)	(40/1,685)
Retained earnings/total assets	**0.27**	**0.26**
(working)	(450/1,675)	(445/1,685)
EBIT/total assets	**0.048**	**0.045**
(working)	(80/1,675)	(75/1,685)
Market cap./total liabilities	**1.5**	**1.75**
(working)	(900/600)	(900/515)
Sales/total assets	**0.60**	**0.56**
(working)	(1,000/1,675)	(950/1,685)

Note that the ratios should be expressed as decimals rather than percentages. This is important when they are input into the Z-score formula (see "magic number" 25B).

CALCULATING THEM FOR
JOLLIBEE

Figure 25.2 shows the various ratios calculated from the 2001 accounts of Jollibee Foods Corporation (JFC). JFC is a Philippines-based fast food retailing company. More information about the group can be found on its web site *www.jolibee.com.ph*.

Figure 25.2   Calculating it for Jollibee Foods Corporation

The figures ...

The following relevant items have been extracted from the accounts of the Jollibee Foods Corporation:

Income statement year to December 31	2001 Phpm	2000 Phpm
Sales	18,789	15,691
EBIT	1,203	1,114

Balance sheet as at December 31		
Stocks	1,089	898
Debtors and prepayments	1,672	1,557
Accounts payable and accrued expenses	2,753	2,541
Working capital	**8**	**−86**
(working)	(1,089 + 1,672 − 2,753)	(898 + 1,557 − 2,541)
Total assets	**10,088**	**8,898**
Reserve for retained earnings	**3,898**	**3,541**
Total liabilities	**4,135**	**3,019**
Shares in issue (m)	957.8	1,008.60
Share price (peso)	18.25	
Market capitalization (PhPm)	**17,480**	
(working)	(18.25 × 957.8)	

The calculations ...

Working capital/total assets is ...	**0.0008**	**−0.0097**
(working)	(8/10,088)	(−86/8,898)
Retained earnings/total assets	**0.386**	**0.398**
(working)	(3,898/10,088)	(3,541/8,898)
EBIT/total assets	**0.119**	**0.125**
(working)	(1,203/10,088)	(1,114/8,898)

Market cap./total liabilities	4.23	5.79
(working)	(17,480/4,135)	(17,480/3,019)
Sales/total assets	1.86	1.76
(working)	(18,789/10,088)	(15,691/8,898)

There are several specific points that need highlighting in these calculations. The first obvious one is that Jollibee has low or negative working capital. This is because as a large fast food operator it can negotiate very favorable terms with suppliers and so effectively finance its business on a day-to-day basis through the credit they extend to it. In all other respects, Jollibee has relatively normal ratios.

Working capital calculations need some care in another respect, too. Because Jollibee has franchises we need to take care which figures we use in the calculation. System-wide sales, for example, are a much larger figure than Jollibee's actual sales, because they include sales through franchisees as well as Jollibee's own outlets. Jollibee receives a license fee from franchisees, rather than the full amount of its sales, so it is the sales figure that includes this license fee item that is the correct one to take.

Payments to and from franchisees also crop up elsewhere in the balance sheet. In the calculations we have, for example, included prepayments in receivables and accrued expenses in accounts payable, because these reflect the impact of the franchising system on the balance sheet.

WHAT THEY MEAN

The significance of the various ratios used as the components of the Z-score calculation is generally rooted in the elements that go to make up the reasons why a company might get into financial distress.

The ratio of working capital to total assets is meant to show whether or not a company is consistently seeing a cash outflow from the business. The theory is that ongoing losses will result in shrinking current assets relative to total assets. As the example shows, however, this is a little difficult to apply in the case of companies that enjoy generous credit terms from suppliers.

The ratio of retained earnings to total assets is a measure of the accumulated amount a company has generated to reinvest in the business. Clearly, the higher this figure the better. The more a company retains the greater its ability to finance capital spending and other essentials from its own internal resources. Companies that have large write-offs will deplete their retained earnings and reduce their Z-score.

The EBIT to total assets ratio is an objective way of measuring return on assets without the size of the firm's borrowings or cash, or the tax regime it operates under, affecting the result.

The ratio of market capitalization to total liabilities shows the extent to which the company's stock market value can decline before the figure drops below the company's liabilities and adds a stock market dimension to the calculation.

The ratio of sales to total assets represents the effectiveness with which management is using the company's assets to generate sales and ultimately cash.

While these may seem to be random ratios, it is when they are weighted in the correct proportions and combined that they provide a test of financial solidity that has proved over the years to be extremely reliable. This is the subject of the next "magic number."

The Z-Score

THE DEFINITION

The Z-score is the total of a number of key ratios drawn from the income statement, balance sheet, and stock market, each of which is assigned a weight to determine its relative importance in the total. The Z-score is generally considered to be an accurate indicator of creditworthiness for mainstream industrial companies.

THE FORMULAS

For *publicly listed* companies:

$$Z = 1.2 \times \text{item 1} + 1.4 \times \text{item 2} + 3.3 \times \text{item 3} + 0.6 \times \text{item 4} + \text{item 5}$$

Where:

Item 1 = working capital/total assets

Item 2 = accumulated retained earnings/total assets

Item 3 = EBIT/total assets

Item 4 = market capitalization/total liabilities

Item 5 = sales/total assets

For *private* companies, different weightings of the same items are used, as below:

$$Z = 6.56 \times \text{item } 1 + 3.26 \times \text{item } 2 + 6.72 \times \text{item } 3 + 1.5 \times \text{item } 4$$

Note here that item 5 is omitted. In item 4 net tangible assets at book value is substituted for market capitalization.

THE COMPONENTS

Working capital/total assets – working capital is normally defined as stocks (or inventories) plus debtors and prepayments (sometimes called receivables), less creditors and accrued expenses (sometimes called accounts payable). Total assets are the sum of fixed assets (including intangible assets where appropriate) and current assets. You calculate the ratio by dividing one item into the other and expressing the result as a decimal.

Accumulated retained earnings/total assets – accumulated retained earnings are sometimes known as the profit and loss account reserve. The item represents the total of retained profits from successive years' income statements. When assets are written down in value, unless reserves have been created specifically for this purpose beforehand, the amount written off will be charged to accumulated retained earnings. Total assets are as defined above. You calculate the ratio by dividing one item into the other and expressing the result as a decimal.

EBIT/total assets – EBIT (earnings before interest and tax) is profit before tax plus interest paid less interest received. Total assets were defined earlier. You calculate the ratio by dividing one item into the other and expressing the result as a decimal.

Market capitalization/total liabilities – market capitalization is shares in issue (in this case at the year-end) multiplied by the price of the shares. Total liabilities are the total of current liabilities, all long-term creditors, and provisions for liabilities and charges. You calculate the ratio by dividing one item into the other and expressing the result as a decimal.

Sales/total assets – net sales are the revenue of the company less any sales taxes. Total assets are as defined above. You calculate the ratio by dividing one item into the other and expressing the result as a decimal.

WHERE'S THE DATA?

Most Z-score data is normally readily available from the face of the balance sheet or income statement. Notes may need to be used, either for clarification or to find out certain other figures.

In the case of *accumulated retained earnings* (profit and loss account reserve), it may be necessary to consult the note to the accounts that refers to share capital and reserves.

EBIT may also need to be worked out using the notes to the accounts to identify the precise amount of interest paid and/or received. This should then be added back to the stated figure for pre-tax profits.

Total assets and *total liabilities* are either stated on the face of the balance sheet or calculated by adding up the relevant numbers and subtotals.

The *market capitalization* calculation may require notes to the accounts to be consulted to determine the year-end shares in issue (normally in the note related to paid-up share capital and reserves), while the share price can be had from the price pages of a normal financial daily paper.

CALCULATING IT – THE THEORY

Figure 25.3 shows the different numbers to be pulled from the accounts, and how to use them to calculate the relevant items and in turn the Z-score.

Figure 25.3   Calculating the "Magic Number" for the Z-score

Bonza Pharma Pty Ltd, an Australian drug company, has the following Z-score components. These have been derived as shown in Figure 25.1.

Year to December 31	2002	2001
1. Working capital/total assets	0.039	0.024
2. Retained earnings/total assets	0.27	0.26
3. EBIT/total assets	0.048	0.045
4. Market cap./total liabilities	1.5	1.75
5. Sales/total assets	0.60	0.56

The formula for the Z-score is:

$Z = 1.2 \times$ item 1 $+ 1.4 \times$ item 2 $+ 3.3 \times$ item 3 $+ 0.6 \times$ item 4 $+$ item 5

In this case the numbers are:

$Z = (1.2 \times 0.039) + (1.4 \times 0.27) + (3.3 \times 0.048) + (0.6 \times 1.5) + 0.6$

Which equates to:

$Z = 0.047 + 0.378 + 0.158 + 0.9 + 0.6$
$Z = 2.083$

This suggests that Bonza Pharma is in a gray area, tending toward financial weakness. Any Z-score between 1.81 and 2.99 is considered in a gray area. Any Z-score below 1.81 is considered unhealthy.

CALCULATING IT FOR

JOLLIBEE

Figure 25.4 shows the Z-score for Jollibee Foods Corporation and how it is derived from the various ratios calculated from the company's 2001 accounts. As recorded in the previous "magic number," JFC is a Philippines-based fast food retailing company. More information about the group is available at its web site *www.jolibee.com.ph*.

Figure 25.4   Calculating it for Jollibee Foods Corporation

The figures (from Figure 25.2) ...

	2001	2000
Working capital/total assets	0.0008	−0.0097
Retained earnings/total assets	0.386	0.398
EBIT/total assets	0.119	0.125
Market cap./total liabilities	4.23	5.79
Sales/total assets	1.86	1.76

The calculations ...

The formula for the Z-score is ...

$Z = 1.2 \times$ item 1 $+ 1.4 \times$ item 2 $+ 3.3 \times$ item 3 $+ 0.6 \times$ item 4 $+$ item 5

In this case the numbers are ...

$Z = (1.2 \times 0.0008) + (1.4 \times 0.386) + (3.3 \times 0.119) + (0.6 \times 4.23) + 1.86$

$Z = 0 + 0.54 + 0.39 + 2.54 + 1.86$

Z = 5.33

The first item is so close to zero it can be ignored. The Z-score of 5.33 suggests Jollibee Foods Company is in an extremely robust financial condition. Any Z-score above 2.99 is considered healthy.

WHAT IT MEANS

The Z-score is a ratio that fell into disuse during the bull market of the 1990s, but is currently undergoing something of a revival. It is easy to see why.

Professor Robert Altman, an American academic, devised the ratio originally during the 1960s, although his innovative work has since been updated to reflect subsequent data. Altman believes that the Z-score will signal 85–90 percent of bankruptcies of publicly listed companies – before they happen.

Both bankers and the more skeptical analysts use the ratio to determine the creditworthiness of particular public and private companies.

Generally speaking, a healthy public company should have a Z of 2.99 or more, an unhealthy one a score of 1.81 or less. For private companies the score for a healthy company would be 2.59 or above, an unhealthy one would have a score of less than 1.1.

There are some drawbacks. The first is that it is generally not suitable for analyzing the accounts of utilities, property companies, banks, insurers, and other financial services companies. A second objection is that relatively new companies with a low level of profitability may not get a high score. The scoring method favors long-established companies. Some of the items used to calculate the ratios – notably sales and working capital items – are capable of manipulation by management.

Nonetheless, calculating the Z-score for the same company from the accounts of successive years can highlight where a company's financial condition is deteriorating. If a company's Z-score has fallen over the course of a year or two from a healthy position to one bordering on the unhealthy category, the shares should be avoided.

By the same token, companies whose Z-score is consistently improving from an unhealthy position may be a good bet for share price recovery.

Finding the Information

This appendix is designed to make it easy for you to find information to calculate these "magic numbers" for stock investors.

We concentrate on several areas:

- financial portals for share prices and basic market data, including market capitalization, earnings per share, and dividend data
- ordering print-based material from companies
- official sources of information
- getting information from company investor relations web sites
- useful spreadsheets and calculators.

Links to all of the sites mentioned are also available at the "magic numbers" web site *www.magicnumbersbook.com*.

FINANCIAL PORTALS

A portal is simply a gateway to the web – a site containing features and links relevant to your interests, a means of searching for information, and other facilities. Many have grown naturally out of "search engines" like AltaVista or Lycos, and some from newspapers. Some are pure start-ups.

However, if you are an active investor, there is a range of specialist financial portals you can use. Some are more relevant than others, but all share common themes.

Most financial portals allow you to access stock market prices on companies. They also feature financial news and bulletin boards, which enable you to interact online with other investors.

Financial portals usually give you access to share price charts and a facility whereby either one or more portfolios or "watch lists" can be monitored. Setting up a list of companies you are interested in following regularly is a good way of monitoring prices and news.

You may need to know the stock market symbols (sometimes called "ticker symbols") in order to set up a "watch list." Sites differ in the ease with which data can be entered and changed. Some sites also allow "watch list" information to be viewed via a mobile device such as a 3G mobile phone or handheld PDA.

Individual company information (including accounts data) is usually also available at financial portals. Sites often link to other financial information and bulletin board comments direct from the quote page.

The following are a few examples of sites that contain comprehensive company or market information that you may find useful.

Bloomberg (*www.bloomberg.com*) has become known for localizing its popular broadcast content for individual markets, and the same is true of its web presence. Design and site layout varies little from market to market, and local languages are frequently used. English-speaking sites can be accessed from *www.bloomberg.co.uk* and *www.bloomberg.com/asia/.*

Market Eye (*www.finexprestel.com/marketeye*) is a subscription-only broadcast real-time data service, covering a wide range of markets. It was originally launched by the Stock Exchange in 1987. A demonstration version is available on the site.

Comdirect's "market focus" section is outstandingly good for snapshots of a wide range of international markets, indices, and their constituents. English speakers can access the site from *www.comdirect.co.uk*. It is not necessary to be a client of the broker to access the site. Markets covered include all of the main ones in Asia, Europe, and North America.

Ample (*www.iii.co.uk*) has prices plus news and commentary. The site also includes model portfolios based on the UK market. For a monthly fee, investors can access "Desktoptrader," which offers monthly prices, LSE trade data, news, broker forecasts, and more.

FTMarketWatch (*www.ftmarketwatch.com*) has comprehensive information on all main global stock markets and the companies within them, including price data and company information, much of which can be used to calculate "magic numbers." Most of the information is available only on subscription.

Good UK-based sites include **ADVFN** (*www.advfn.com*). This has free real-time prices for UK stocks and the usual complement of portal accoutrements, including active bulletin boards.

Yahoo! Finance has a range of local language sites in various international markets with a broadly similar offering in each, focused around financial news and standardized company information. Start from *http://finance.yahoo.com*.

Specifically Asian portals include **Quamnet** (*www.quamnet.com*), which has real-time quotes, charts, news, and a daily market commentary. It offers analysis and extensive news coverage in different industrial sectors, and it also has a page devoted to investor tools. Launched in 1998 in Hong Kong, the site also features a list of contributing columnists, some of whom can be emailed with comments and suggestions.

Wallstraits (*www.wallstraits.com*) offers a wealth of free information. Prices, charts, and financial highlights for each company can be easily accessed. A weekly update of all new content and features is available by email together with IR alerts for individual companies. The online school section offers courses on investment that are free following registration.

Shareinvestor (*www.shareinvestor.com*) has prices, charts, 30-minute delayed news, portfolio tracking, and company snapshots. Some information is free and a guest membership is available. There is a useful link from the site to *www.listedcomany.com*. This site provides corporate and financial information, news, webcasts, and email alerts for 75 listed Singapore companies.

Netresearch (*www.netresearch-asia.com*) provides independent research on companies in Asia and Singapore, some of which is free. A link is provided to the Singapore Stock Exchange for live prices.

Surf88 (*www.surf88.com*) provides free information such as news and analysis, articles, shareholder tracking, and an investment tutorial. It is necessary to register. Other services such as detailed fundamental analysis are available on subscription.

Information on the Malaysian markets can also be found at **TA Enterprise Berhad** (*www.ta.com.my*). The site offers a free daily market commentary with further research and information available to account holders.

IDS Finance (*www.idsfinance.com*) has a free service that includes analysts' reports, company summaries, historical price charts, and market news. In addition, subscribers can access real-time stock quotes, news, charts, and investment tools plus financial analysis covering six countries and nine exchanges across the region.

Australian financial information can be found at **Stockhouse** (*www.stockhouse.au*). The site has news, company profiles, brokerage reports, bulletin boards, and portfolio tracking. Membership is free with an optional subscription to email services such as portfolio updates.

ORDERING PRINT-BASED INFORMATION

Companies are generally duty bound to send annual accounts to their shareholders. They will also often send them to other investors who may be interested. A telephone call to the company secretary or the investor relations department at the company, or even simply to their telephone receptionist, should allow you to order one easily.

Many company web sites now contain the email address of the company's investor relation officials. A spreadsheet containing a list of leading UK, European, and US companies that offer this facility is available at *www.magicnumbersbook.com*.

A simple email asking for an "investor pack" or a copy of the latest accounts and that provides your postal address should suffice.

World Investor Link (WIL) is an independent organization that operates in conjunction with leading business newspapers around the world to mail out copies of participating companies' annual reports free of any charge to anyone that requests them. You can find contact details for WIL in your local business newspaper or the *Financial Times* and *Wall Street Journal*. Reports can be ordered by telephone, fax, by mail, or from WIL's web site at *www.wilink.com*.

Once your details are entered, provided you use the same computer, they need not be resubmitted each time you order a new set of accounts. Material is dispatched (if in stock) within a couple of days. This is an excellent system, although as yet few Asian companies appear to participate.

INFORMATION FROM OFFICIAL SITES

Government company registration organizations, such as the SEC in the United States and Britain's Companies House, are increasingly moving to collect and disseminate data electronically.

The United States is much further along this road than anyone else. The **EDGAR** site (Electronic Data Gathering of Annual Returns) is available at *www.sec.gov/edgarhp.htm*.

Here files can be downloaded free of charge and it is easy to use with plenty of online help. There are also some unofficial Edgar sites such as **Edgar-Online** (*www.edgar-online.com*). This has over 2 million Edgar filings that have been filed with the SEC from 1994 to the present day. It is subscription only.

The UK's **Companies House** now allows online ordering of company accounts returns (covering two years) online at its web site at *www.companieshouse.gov.uk* for £5 each, payable by credit card. The documents can then be downloaded and printed.

Elsewhere, several stock exchange sites also contain links to the accounts data of listed companies. A list of the larger stock exchanges can be found at the "markets" page of the author's web site at *www.linksitemoney.com.*

Asian-orientated sites with detailed company information include:

AnnualReport.com.hk (*www.annualreport.com.hk*), where subscribers can obtain annual reports and various other services, all for Hong Kong-listed companies.

For free information **Finet** (*www.e-finet.com*) is a useful site. It offers company profiles, business reviews and recent announcements, condensed annual report statements, and analysis.

Information on Australian companies can be found at the Australian Securities and Investment Commission. The web address is *www.asic.gov.au.*

GETTING INFORMATION VIA COMPANY WEB SITES

Company web sites have increasingly been used by more enlightened companies as a way of disseminating information to shareholders, the press, and other interested parties. Many sites contain a wide range of data, including annual reports available for downloading or viewing online, details of presentations made to analysts, news releases, share price information and price charts, and a range of other information.

Company web sites vary a lot in quality. A summary of the data available for the companies used as examples in this book are given in the Table A.1. A list of company web site addresses for leading US, UK, and European companies can be found at *www.magicnumbersbook.com.* Links to these sites are also available at the author's web site at *www.linksitecorporate.com.*

Company sites have generally been streamlined over the years, abandoning, in the main, the unnecessary gimmicks of earlier versions. Information is presented in a straightforward format with clear opening pages, site maps, and easy navigation.

Let's review quickly the sites of the companies used as examples in the "magic number" calculations. Some sites, such as Altria and Sony, have particularly good home pages, containing relevant investor information at a glance. These include the latest share price, news, and a link to the annual report.

Most of the sites have live share prices and share price charts, with the exception of Jollibee, Hutchison Whampoa, and WPP. The latter does, however, have a link to Bloomberg for this purpose.

Many of the sites feature a FAQ section. This usually covers general investor queries. If a question cannot be answered here it is often possible to email the question to a person on the investor relations team. Some companies allow this. Of the ones used as examples in this book, GlaxoSmithKline, Sony, Hutchison Whampoa, and Singtel have yet to offer this service. In addition, however, CLP has an extra FAQ topic section. This covers areas such as future financial plans and company structure.

All the sites have online annual reports and other results information. It is also usually possible to order the printed report online. McDonald's has interactive financial highlights in two easy-to-use formats. The first has interactive graphs of certain key financial data, such as sales and operating income, while the second includes financial statements, operating results, and an 11-year summary of key financial highlights.

All the sites include press releases and many have email news alerts for which it is possible to register whether or not you are a shareholder. In addition, Microsoft has a monthly investor newsletter and Statoil produces an online magazine three times a year.

Altria has a fact book available for the 2002 financial year that contains financial information. The site also has a useful page that encapsulates the financial performance at a glance, and includes shareholder and dividend information, income statement data and some ratios. Archived speeches can also be viewed.

Webcasts of such events, such as AGMs and analyst presentations, are available on some sites. BAE, Amazon, Microsoft, and McDonald's all offer these.

Microsoft produces an investor pack with a selection of financial and corporate material to download for new investors. The site also features a downloadable tool in Microsoft Excel to help you forecast the forthcoming income statement for yourself.

Useful Spreadsheets and Calculators

A summary ratio analysis calculator can be found at the *Magic Numbers* web site (*www.magicnumbersbook.com*), as can the models for discounted cash flow analysis, reinvested return on equity, and Z-score, and some other ratios referred to in the book. These spreadsheets require Excel 5 or higher.

These and a range of other spreadsheets and links to downloadable investment software covering charting, option pricing, personal financial management, and other topics can also be found on the "software" page at the author's web site *www.linksitemoney.com*.

Table A.1   Type of information available on web sites of companies discussed in this book

Company	URL	Annual reports available	Results info. available	Other press releases	Presenta-tions	"Live" share price contact	Share price chart	Investor relations email	Country of origin
Glaxo	www.gsk.com	Yes	Yes	Yes	Yes	Yes	Yes	No	UK
Sony	www.sony.net	Yes	Yes	Yes	Yes	Yes	Yes	No	US
Altria	www.altria.com	Yes	Yes	Yes	No	Yes	Yes	Yes	US
Statoil	www.statoil.com	Yes	Yes	Yes	Yes	Yes	Yes	Yes	Norway
Microsoft	www.microsoft.com	Yes	Yes	Yes	Yes	Yes	Yes	Yes	US
McDonald's	www.mcdonalds.com	Yes	Yes	Yes	No	Yes	Yes	Yes	US
Hutchison Whampoa	www.hutchison-whampoa.com	Yes	Yes	Yes	No	No	No	No	Hong Kong
BAE	www.baesystems.com	Yes	Yes	Yes	Yes	Yes	Yes	Yes	UK
GE	www.ge.com	Yes	Yes	Yes	Yes	Yes	No	Yes	US
WPP	www.wpp.com	Yes	Yes	Yes	Yes	No	No	Yes	UK
Amazon	www.amazon.com	Yes	Yes	Yes	No	Yes	Yes	Yes	US
CLP Holdings	www.clpgroup.com	Yes	Yes	Yes	Yes	Yes	Yes	Yes	Hong Kong
Singtel	www.singtel.com	Yes	Yes	Yes	Yes	Yes	Yes	No	Singapore
Jollibee	www.jollibee.com	Yes	Yes	Yes	No	No	No	Yes	Philippines

Index